The Artful Home

The Artful Home

Using Art & Craft to Create Living Spaces You'll Love

Toni Sikes
Founder of The Guild

LARK BOOKS

A Division of
Sterling Publishing Co., Inc.
New York / London

Library of Congress Cataloging-in-Publication Data

Sikes, Toni Fountain.
   The artful home : using art & craft to create living spaces you'll love /
Toni Sikes. -- 1st ed.
       p. cm.
   Includes index.
   ISBN-13: 978-1-60059-171-6 (hc-plc with jacket : alk. paper)
   ISBN-10: 1-60059-171-X (hc-plc with jacket : alk. paper)
   1. Handicraft. 2. House furnishings. 3. Interior decoration. I. Title.
TT157.S528 2007
747'.5--dc22

                              2007007176

10 9 8 7 6 5 4 3 2 1

First Edition

Published by Lark Books, A Division of
Sterling Publishing Co., Inc.
387 Park Avenue South, New York, N.Y. 10016

© 2007, The Guild, Inc.

Distributed in Canada by Sterling Publishing,
c/o Canadian Manda Group, 165 Dufferin Street
Toronto, Ontario, Canada M6K 3H6

Distributed in the United Kingdom by GMC Distribution Services,
Castle Place, 166 High Street, Lewes, East Sussex, England BN7 1XU

Distributed in Australia by Capricorn Link (Australia) Pty Ltd.,
P.O. Box 704, Windsor, NSW 2756 Australia

The written instructions, photographs, designs, patterns, and projects in this volume are intended for
the personal use of the reader and may be reproduced for that purpose only. Any other use, especially
commercial use, is forbidden under law without written permission of the copyright holder.

Every effort has been made to ensure that all the information in this book is accurate. However, due to
differing conditions, tools, and individual skills, the publisher cannot be responsible for any injuries,
losses, and other damages that may result from the use of the information in this book.

If you have questions or comments about this book, please contact:
Lark Books
67 Broadway
Asheville, NC 28801
(828) 253-0467

Manufactured in China

ISBN 13: 978-1-60059-171-6
ISBN 10: 1-60059-171-X

For information about custom editions, special sales, premium and corporate purchases, please contact
Sterling Special Sales Department at 800-805-5489 or specialsales@sterlingpub.com.

SENIOR EDITOR:
Valerie Van Arsdale Shrader

PROJECT EDITOR/CONTRIBUTING WRITER:
Jill Schaefer

CONTRIBUTING WRITER:
Melita Schuessler

ART DIRECTOR:
Kristi Pfeffer

COVER DESIGNER:
Cindy LaBreacht

ASSOCIATE EDITOR:
Nathalie Mornu

ASSOCIATE ART DIRECTOR:
Shannon Yokeley

ART PRODUCTION ASSISTANT:
Jeff Hamilton

EDITORIAL ASSISTANCE:
Cassie Moore

COVER PHOTOGRAPHY:
Eric Ferguson
(front cover, front flap, back cover [top,
bottom center, and bottom right], back
flap, and spine)
Jonas Gerard
(back cover [bottom left])
Stephen Funk
(author photo, back flap)

The Artful Home

Welcome 9

Creating the Artful Home 11
Developing a Personal Style 12
Learning to See 15
Think Like an Artist 20

The Art of Composition 24
Understanding Design Principles 26
Creating Vignettes 32
Finding a Focal Point 36
Playing with Scale 39
Adding Texture and Material 40
Appreciating Geometry 42

The Character of Color 45
Living in Color 46
Exploring Color: A Primer 50
The Art of White Walls 54

Living with Beautiful Objects 56
Dressing Your Home's Intimate Spaces 58
Decorating Creatively 62
Establishing Relationships 64
Opportunities for Display 66
Displaying Small Treasures 73
Adding a Showstopper 74

Decorating Walls and Floors 77
Bringing Walls to Life 78
Arranging Artwork 83
Finding Neutral Ground 89
Styling Your Floor 95
Selecting Floor Coverings 96

Guide to the Artful Home, Room by Room 98

The Entryway 101
The Living Room 103
The Dining Room 112
The Bedroom 115
The Bathroom 118
Regarding Furniture 121

Acquiring and Protecting Artful Objects 127

Finding Art 128
Commissioning Artwork 131

Determining Value 133
Collecting Artful Objects 135
Care and Maintenance of Your Artwork 138

In Conclusion 142
Art Glossary 143
Artist Credits 148
Design Professional Credits 154
Photo Credits 156
Acknowledgments 157
Index 158

"I like to think of the homemaking process
as a journey, one without beginning or end,
limited only by my time and imagination."

Welcome

The creation of an artful home is a journey, one without beginning or end, limited only by time and imagination. I developed this notion from my mother, who taught me to focus on the details in our daily lives. She showed me how to use tiny stitches when hemming a skirt so that it wouldn't bunch up and would instead last forever. She insisted that, when we had hamburgers for dinner, we put the mustard and ketchup in bowls on the table, never in the jars they came in! And that cloth napkins were oh-so-much better than paper napkins, and should be used every day. Why? Because every day is just as important as a holiday.

Our middle-class home wasn't fancy, but it was filled with fresh cut flowers, needle-pointed pillows, home-baked cakes, and antiques from shops and flea markets. By paying attention to the details, my mother showed me that life was all about making the ordinary into the extraordinary.

When I grew up and left home, I realized that her lessons manifested themselves in the things I chose to have around me. Without knowing when or why, I had come to cherish beauty, and to love a thing well made. So I was naturally attracted to the work of artists in every medium.

It was through art that I discovered the stuff that dreams are made of—beautiful paintings, remarkable sculpture, works in ceramic, glass, wood, and fiber. The work of artists spoke to me without the baggage of verbs and nouns, and many pieces seemed to express my heart's deepest yearnings.

Today, my home has become the repository for all this beautiful stuff that I have gathered over the years. It has steered me into a lifelong search for ways to display, arrange, rearrange, and live with the art that I love.

I'm presumptuous enough to believe that you, too, are on a similar journey to create a home that suits your individual needs, reflects your personality, and soothes your soul. It is out of this presumption that this book, *The Artful Home*, is born. In these pages, I seek to be your helpful guide as you create your own artful home. Thank you for joining me on the journey.

Toni Sikes

Creating *the* Artful Home

What is the artful home? It's not just a house full of paintings. It's an inviting hallway inhabited by an imaginative chair, a collection of beloved teapots, or a mixture of art on the walls and objects on the shelves. These ingredients, which reveal thought, personality, and sense of style, combine to create a very special feeling for those who live there and those who visit.

The secret to creating an artful home is to think like an artist, drawing upon the design concepts used by the professionals to transform environments into special places. Artists use color, composition, form, texture, pattern, and materials to express their ideas and emotions.

Approach your home as a painter would approach his canvas, using composition to arrange the elements at your disposal. Look to color and form to create beauty and interest. Then, turn to texture and pattern to build character, harmony, and visual focus. Think of design concepts as guidelines—tools in your toolbox. Above all, learn to trust your eye and intuition.

The purpose of this book is to help you create your own artful home. I begin by encouraging you to develop and become more aware of your own personal aesthetic. Then, after identifying key design concepts, I discuss how to use these concepts to incorporate objects and artwork into the home environment. I conclude with a room-by-room guide and then offer specific ideas for acquiring works of art that suit your unique vision.

Creating the artful home is a journey that takes time and thought, so slow down and enjoy the process. Inevitably, you will create special spaces that shape you as much as you shape them.

think like an artist

Developing a Personal Style

As we search for a sanctuary in this fast-paced world, we look homeward to find it. The home has taken on new significance as we spend increasing amounts of time there—enjoying family, entertaining friends, sometimes working, and often just relaxing.

We live in a cookie-cutter world, yet each of us has different, complicated psychic needs and tastes. The contemporary home provides something beyond a simple refuge; it's the place where we express our individual sense of style, put our stamp, inscribe our personal signature.

As we seek to develop living spaces that are designed to articulate a personality rather than adhere to a systematic decorating style, we look to artists for inspiration. Today, a growing nucleus of artists and artisans is creating exciting products for the home. They're producing work that is made of traditional materials using traditional techniques, as well as pieces crafted with unexpected materials in innovative ways. The mark of the human hand draws us back to values believed to be lost, and guides us away from the trendy in search of the enduring.

Handmade objects—ceramic wall sconce, glass vase, books, and small bronze sculpture—speak volumes about this home's owner. The mixture of eclectic elements creates visual interest while suggesting a thoughtful yet casual lifestyle.

A room with unadorned windows and little architectural detail becomes an intimate sanctuary with the addition of a luminous column, a rich black and wine-red color palette, and luxurious textures on floors and furnishings.

Through their work, intensely individualistic and constantly evolving, artists conspire to help us find our own personal style. They provide a cornucopia of home furnishings—from the glass candlesticks on the dining room table, to the quilt on the bed, to the painting hanging on the wall—with which to express ourselves in the rooms of our homes. In their creations, we re-discover the love of materials, the joy of singularity, the pleasure of things well made.

Perhaps more importantly, artists and their artwork inspire us as we create home spaces marked with our personal signature style. Experimental by nature, artists challenge us with fresh, new thinking about design elements that help us define and refine our own tastes. We look to them to stimulate our senses and help us imagine the possibilities.

As I was writing this book, I found myself returning, time and again, to my personal journal. Over the years, this journal is the place where I've captured my thoughts about art, beauty, creativity, and home. I share these reflections throughout the book in entries called "Just a Thought."

just *a thought*

Remember when former American president Jimmy Carter famously confessed that he had lust in his heart? Well, let me confess that there is lust in my heart… for hefty salad bowls and coffee mugs that make my hand want to linger. For colored glass vases that are as beautiful as the tulips they hold. For glowing lamps that change the atmosphere of a room, and paintings that transport me out of the room to somewhere else entirely. For handmade furniture and rugs, teapots and pitchers, sculpture and objects, and oh so much more.

These things hold a power over me that I cannot explain. I wake every morning to this David Moose painting of sky and clouds on my bedroom wall, and the day is off to just the right start.

I no longer feel guilty about the fact that I covet beautiful things. I am at peace with this lust in my heart! Perhaps the Irish poet Thomas Moore says it best: "We work with the stuff of the soul by means of the things of life."

Learning
To See

Home is the one place in your life that is uniquely yours. Whether it is a one-bedroom apartment in the city or a sprawling country estate, this space reflects who you are, where you come from, and how you got there. In order to better express your unique sense of style, you want to develop a personal aesthetic—the value system that defines your individual sense of beauty, grace, and comfort. This requires learning to see, to look with a new eye at your surroundings. It means coming to terms with the fact that everything in your living environment—from the paint color on the walls to the place mats on the table—blend and work together to make your life richer.

A personal aesthetic develops from building a point of view about space, proportions, and texture. I find that I can refine that point of view by identifying colors, patterns, and the types of art that are meaningful to me. For instance, I love ornament and rough surfaces,

This dining room wall piece invites a dialogue. Color, texture, pattern, and symbols drop visual clues that draw the viewer in for closer inspection.

while others insist on simple lines and clean surfaces. I also prefer warm, intimate rooms filled with great pottery; a friend favors bright, airy spaces that show off her glass collection. This exercise takes practice and matures over time, but once I develop the aesthetic values that are meaningful to me, I can use those values in the design and content of my home. When you consider the architecture of your living environment, the array of furnishings you select, and the art you acquire, you should be able to recognize how these pieces work together to balance the many elements of design: composition, color, and texture.

Creating a personal aesthetic also involves cultivating a point of view with regard to material possessions. It means looking at things in different ways in order to generate new perspectives. The Japanese believe that "to see" an art object, one must go directly to the core of the object.

Strong color is the quickest attention-getter in decoration, a sure-fire way to direct the eye. On this mantle, the print and sculpture stand out against a neutral background. The giant glass jacks call one to take a second look at the subject matter of this clever print.

Learning to see requires that you look at many objects and absorb what each one has to offer. You can accomplish this by developing a dialogue with an object. No, I don't mean speaking out loud to it, but rather becoming curious about it. Where is it from? How old is it? Was it crafted by hand or by machine? What unusual techniques were used to produce it? Did its creator sign it? How does this piece make you feel? Finding the answers to these questions will enrich your understanding and deepen your appreciation of the object you're looking at. This process increases your knowledge, strengthens your personal aesthetic, and prepares your eye to seek beauty in all that it sees.

When you introduce art into your home, you're adding a layer onto a foundation established through the furnishings, lighting, and accessories that you've inherited or purchased over time. These possessions were doubtless acquired as much for their function as for taste and style. Creating an artful home is about selecting and placing art that complements your core furnishings while celebrating beauty and spirit and reflecting something intimate about you and your family.

Looking at art feels very different from looking at other kinds of furnishings. An artist's work can take you by surprise. It can inspire pleasure, confusion, or an immediate sense of affinity. You may like what you're looking at, or you may not. Either way, your eye is stimulated, and the piece calls to you for response and reaction.

Buying art for your home involves a different set of standards than those faced by a museum. The right surroundings and appropriate placement in your home environment are much more important than investment appeal. Ultimately, your passion for a work of art should always drive your purchase. This is one area where you should lead with your heart.

Personal signatures carry elements of surprise. Unexpected details including carved edges, high-contrast hand-painting, and jazzy upholstery animate these chairs, expressing the quirks of their creator and, by extension, their current owner.

"Use My Art"

The artist who conspires to help us create our own personal signature also says, "Use my art." The hand-woven rug is, of course, beautiful and beautifully made and could be hung on the wall and viewed as a painting. But the rug was made to be walked on, to warm floors, and to soothe tired feet; it invites us to sit on it with friends, to wrestle on it with grandchildren. Its beauty enhances, rather than interferes, with its function.

Coordination of color in this living room comes from the partnership of the large painting with the console table and the objects on it. The cool greens of the painting are picked up by the painted outline of the furniture and the teapot set. Hot tones in orange and red serve as accents in the lamp and wall color.

The painted gold interior of these teacups fulfills a decorative function in the simplest possible way. The slash of color provides a visual separation between the inside and outside of the cup, bringing these plain but elegant objects to life.

The artist-made teapot and teacups have a quiet beauty. When not in use, these objects can be displayed with pride on the living room console. They stand in their own space and command respect in the room. But, ultimately, the teapot and teacups are made to be used. Filled with a fragrant tea, the teapot serves a warm drink that delights and sustains. The teacups dance across the countertop, asking to be picked up. Whether for functional use, quiet contemplation, or purely sensual beauty, the teapot and teacups are products of the artist's devotion to and expansion of an ageless art form.

The floor is no longer just a bland background on which furniture resides. These days, artists are creating paintings for the floor out of fiber and canvas. In this grand entry room, the staircase boldly sweeps down to a large, colorful rug that is set against a backdrop of white painted walls. The dramatic colors of the rug are carried through in all of the art used in the room.

Personal expression and comfort are the twin priorities of this relaxed sitting area. Artwork and objects that appear to have been assembled over time find a home amid warm colors, soft textiles, and furnishings with a patina of age.

Think Like an Artist

I often think of my home as a white canvas; the rooms are empty and the spaces are filled with natural light. I do this mental exercise because, in reality, my home is like yours: not perfect. Cats, too much clutter, things to throw away. I like to close my eyes and mentally empty the space of everything, starting over from scratch. Just dreaming about the possibilities puts me in a better mood.

Like an artist, I begin to gather ideas and let them accumulate over time. For this purpose, I have a favorite set of markers and a three-ring binder with pockets. This notebook provides a single place to collect things like inspirational magazine clippings, paint chips, and fabric swatches. I have an active imagination and like to change my mind a lot. Photos and sketches help me develop my aesthetic on paper, where it's easy to try different options. I begin to have a better understanding of what I like and don't like.

Take Your Time

As you become more artful in your approach to your home, slow down and enjoy the process of getting there. In a world where so much is results-driven, projects at home need not be rushed. Take time to visualize home spaces that are new and refreshing. Because we are inundated by stuff—cool stuff, fun stuff, useful stuff, junk—there are so many judgments to make. As I've grown older, I find that I don't want a lot of things. But I do want the right things. The things that excite me.

I've learned that if you want to find out what really makes your blood pump, you have to slow down, look closely, and listen. My heart pounds loudest for authentic things that speak of the work of the hand, and pulse with the energy of their creation. Too many objects

Draw attention to prints and photographs by placing them on a background of colored walls. In this hallway, the light blue wall color introduces warmth and brightness as well as showcases the two prints. Here, almost everything else in the hall is white, wood-toned, or neutral, keeping competition between the other elements at bay. The intriguing bench adds enduring charm.

You can put two or more strong patterns in the same piece of furniture as long as they have equivalent weights. Here, the pattern on the table front is just as robust as the pattern on the side slats on the table and mirror. The horizontal lines of the table work well with treasured art books on the floor.

This wall mural makes a playful backdrop for outdoor meals. With zest, flashes of yellow on the tabletop and a trio of real lemons elaborate on one of the artist's themes.

today speak only of efficiency, uniformity, and surface seduction. These things may make a contribution to my daily life, but I can't say I treasure them. Why not? I think it has a lot to do with how easily they can be replaced.

Artists, on the other hand, design their work to be kept forever. They want their pieces to take on the patina that comes from years of being touched. The artist trusts the process of making—accidents included—rather than imposing an artificial uniformity. The artist engages in an ongoing dialogue with materials and techniques instead of engineering rules to force the variables into submission. Rather than assuming control, the artist opens a channel of communication with the material and prepares to have a conversation.

The sparks generated by that conversation are possibility, discovery, something unforeseen. The resulting objects are the product of an individual testing his or her abilities and renewing the act of creation.

I want to support that effort. Living with the objects made by artists reminds me who I am, and what I value. It helps me make a home that reflects me. I am making the statement, "This is not just mine. This is me." Take time to look at art and to think about the kind of artwork you want to live with. Learn about the artists whose work speaks to you, about their inspirations and their techniques. This knowledge trains your eyes and enriches your personal aesthetic. It helps expand and strengthen your point of view, and develop your personal signature style.

Tips for Thinking Like an Artist

When you think about your home, think like an artist. Artists are curious individuals who are driven by a desire to create and a willingness to take chances. They have a special way of seeing and thinking about the world, which is shared with others through the works they create. Here are some tips to help you get into an artistic frame of mind:

- Dream and fantasize about the possibilities. Shelter magazines offer endless ideas, the stuff of dreams!

- Mimicry is a great way to develop your design skills. Tear out photos of beautiful rooms you find in magazines. Browse, instead of shop, through home furnishings catalogs. This frees your imagination to really see what is appealing to you, without the urgency of need.

- Use home repair, fabric, and art supply stores as an opportunity to familiarize yourself with materials of all sorts, from metal and wood to paper, clay, and paint.

- Become opinionated about what you see. Whenever you visit someone else's house, think about what you like and don't like.

- Arrange furniture, art, and objects in new and interesting ways. Show off your books in places other than bookshelves—on chairs and stools, under tables.

- Don't limit your use of color, or feel like colors must match. (The soul is not beige, after all. It is more a Joseph's coat.)

- Mismatching and eclecticism are not only permitted, they are encouraged. Place flea market finds and personal photos side by side with pieces purchased at galleries.

- Engage your senses. Enjoy the luscious texture of a cashmere throw, the smell of oriental incense, the sound of your favorite Miles Davis CD. Touch, smell, and sound merge with the visual to create a total experience.

- Find beauty in everyday things. Buy a hefty coffee mug made by a potter, and start every day with this small piece of art.

just *a thought*

Daffodils are my favorite flower. My grandmother grew them, so they remind me of her and my childhood, especially the long summer weeks she and I spent together.

Each spring, I have the luxury of watching several varieties of daffodils grow right outside my door, which means that these beautiful flowers, memory laden, find their way inside my home on a regular basis.

The association with memories is a constant theme with so many of the favorite things with which we surround ourselves, whether it's treasured family photos or a quilt passed down through the generations. Intuitively, we seek out objects and artwork that have meaning, connection, and transcendence for us. The color yellow or the image of a daffodil transports me in time, the same way a torn page from my favorite travel book to Italy does.

Oscar Wilde wrote, "Memory is the diary that we all carry about with us." Even when literal daffodils aren't available, my glass vase with daffodils serves as a bookmark in my own personal diary of memories.

It isn't the things that make a home; what makes a home is the loving spirit in which those things are gathered. In the process of gathering, we happily re-connect with the people and times that have made us who we are today.

The Art *of* Composition

Human eyes scan their environment, picking up and filing away thousands of seemingly unconnected details. Behind those eyes, the mind works diligently, seeking and identifying patterns and creating a complex web of associations.

We often credit artists with seeing more—and more deeply—than the rest of us. Whether they come by their powers of perception through birth, formal training, or years of practice, artists see details keenly and, beyond that, they find patterns and meanings in those details that elude others. To share these insights, they must, in turn, find ways to shape, sharpen, and shift the perceptions of those who encounter their work. This effort requires artists to use their command of compositional elements to tell stories, present multiple points of view, and, at times, ask open-ended questions.

When you begin to view your home as a composition and strive to fit all of its pieces together in a meaningful way, you, too, are thinking like an artist. As always, the elements of the composition depend on the chosen medium. A painter thinks in terms of line. A sculptor manipulates shape and space. Both artists make decisions about color and light, texture and material. In an artful home, all of these compositional elements come into play.

Recognizing that a particular color or the sculptural shape of a chair inspires and pleases you is the first step. Next, you have to figure out how those tangerine-colored walls will live with everything else going on in your kitchen and whether your very contemporary accent chair can coexist with the dining room set you inherited from your grandparents. With sharp eyes and a sense of adventure, you will find that almost anything can be arranged.

sharp eyes and a sense of adventure

Understanding
Design Principles

Great design puts many different elements together in a way that makes visual, practical, and emotional sense. At home, artwork and special pieces need to live comfortably with the flotsam of our daily lives—the books just finished or about to be read, the flowers recently picked from the garden, the tools we use to prepare our meals. Push and pull between decorative flourishes and realities of life in progress make our spaces feel comfortable, warm, and well lived in.

Ultimately, great design strives for unity. The success of an individual room or the home as a whole is expressed in its overall coherence. This is not a state of perfect order defined according to some objective standard. Instead, it is the deeply satisfying impression that everything fits together, animated by an inner logic.

Our homes are ever-changing still lifes, built on a foundation of line, shape, color, and texture. Intuitively or consciously, we set these compositional elements in motion using the design principles described below. They are not rules but concepts to consider, ways of thinking about compositional relationships.

Variety

The eye delights in variety. Without it, our homes and lives would be studies in unrelieved monotony. Variety implies contrast, and this is essential to creating and holding visual interest. Too much variety breeds chaos, however; points of contrast should support a home's overall design coherence without detracting from its comfort.

just *a thought*

Over the years, I've struggled to articulate my feelings about art, beauty, beautiful art, and why, oh why, we need to have these things in our lives. Beauty in art is so complicated and mysterious that it defies explanation, and yet is so simple and straightforward that most recognize it immediately, intuitively.

A beautiful still life, for instance, does not so much appeal to the intellect as it does to the spirit. In doing so, it transcends the ordinariness of its subject matter and becomes something far more profound.

I believe that beauty is as significant and important in our everyday lives as it is in works of art. At home, a thing of beauty—be it a magnificent table, a vase of daffodils, or a black-and-white photograph—provides daily nourishment for the soul.

Variety. This eclectic group confidently pairs bold geometric shapes in the painting and on the ceramic vessel with whimsical figurative details—dogs racing across the table's apron and flowers blooming on the pale walls. Touches of dramatic black throughout define and pull together this vignette.

Emphasis

Many paintings, prints, or photographs have a focal point—an area of significance that compels attention and leads the way into the work of art. Well-planned rooms have focal points, too. Often, an object or work of art may call attention because of its unmistakable beauty and prominent placement, but you can use emphasis to downplay aspects of a room or an object that you don't like as much. For example, a bright coat of paint turns a chest of drawers into a room-changing focal point—and, at the same time, masks the fact that its form and construction are nothing special. The focal point is only as strong as its supporting cast, however. When the rest of the room echoes and elaborates on themes it has introduced, it gains emotional force.

Emphasis. Vivid stained glass mounted in the center of a large window claims immediate attention, then guides the eye toward additional pieces of jewel-toned art glass placed in an otherwise neutral room.

Balance. A long woven runner of bright colors and strong contrasts provides just enough visual ballast for the forceful paintings in this hallway gallery.

Balance

An artful home strikes a complex, resilient balance between many competing elements: spatial characteristics, intended functions, and personalities of inhabitants, to name just a few. In terms of its outward appearance, the goal is to establish an interesting and ultimately comfortable distribution of objects and compositional elements. Balance has an elastic quality—it includes but stretches beyond strict symmetry and matched sets. Asymmetrical balance, for example, describes equilibrium between objects that differ physically but possess a similar visual weight. Generally, the larger or darker an object is, the greater its visual weight.

Rhythm

Musical rhythm unspools through time, calling bodies to dance. Visual rhythm arranges objects, colors, themes, or other compositional elements in space, leading eyes around the room. Rhythm is cumulative—it relies on repetition and contrast for effect.

Rhythm. The surface decoration on a large ceramic vessel sets the rhythm for a larger composition. Incised vertical lines use their inherent strength to lead eyes up and down the walls of the vessel. The same vessel also has two horizontal bands, echoed by the carvings on the legs of the console table, that counter the force of the vertical lines. The undulating band around the vessel's widest point is a sensual touch that relieves the rigorous linear composition.

From pinstripes to expansive florals, fabric patterns have predictable rhythms. In a room, rhythms tend to evolve in a less precise fashion. Think of the interplay between shapes that are similar, but not identical—polka-dotted pillows, round coffee table, and globe-shaped vases build on one another to establish a subtle theme. Color palettes often progress rhythmically throughout an entire home. The rich red that dominates the dining room walls reappears in throw pillows that punctuate the guest bedroom.

Proportion and Scale

Proportion and scale both address relationships of size. Proportion refers to the relationship between a part of an object and the whole, while scale captures the relationships of different objects to one another. As a matter of proportion, large spaces generally demand large furnishings and objects. Large objects have their place in smaller settings, too—an oversized focal point will make the room feel bigger and bolder.

Proportion and scale. Life-size figures cartwheel across wall and ceiling, creating an exuberant focal point that fills the entire room with color and energy.

Using *Negative Space*

Artists understand the value of negative space within a two- or three-dimensional composition. The outline of each positive shape always defines the negative space around it. Our eyes often read the positive shape more easily, but they always register both positive and negative.

The language of positive and negative space, which is also the language of sculpture, offers an intriguing way to think about the artful home. When a sculptor sees a stone, she starts to imagine the form contained within. Try looking at the rooms of your home in the same way.

Creating interesting interior spaces is, first of all, about creating volumes, shapes, and forms. Managing these design elements is fundamental in determining how any interior design project will ultimately work.

The negative space between objects creates its own powerful drama. Given plenty of room to breathe, each individual piece gains significance. These calm, empty areas in a design provide a kind of aesthetic punctuation. They emphasize what is important and show us how to visually read an environment and understand the larger picture.

The lesson of negative space: It is not necessary to pack rooms with things on top of things. Quiet spaces speak as eloquently as objects themselves.

Striking metal shelves create spatial voids that are far from dull. Even the empty spaces fascinate, while others create offbeat frames for the sculptural objects within.

Creating Vignettes

Whether you're decorating a home from scratch or trying to refresh tired decor, starting small is an excellent way to free your imagination.

Decorating a small area requires a keen eye so that every element shines. Even beauty on a palatial scale hinges on small harmonies hiding inside the big picture. Interior designers use the word *vignette* to describe a small scene or composition within a larger design. These small, focused arrangements deftly establish a mood, explore a theme, or tell a story.

There's no formula for creating a successful vignette—no magic number of objects to include, no preferred setting. Possible places for vignettes in your home include, but are not limited to, the area around a fireplace, an entryway, a reading nook, or a dining room buffet. Forgo the fussy and formal, for vignettes offer a chance to showcase a point of view, and, perhaps, a sense of humor.

Build a vignette around something you love, such as an original painting, a beautifully woven basket, or a chair created by an artist. Don't be shy about finding inspiration in the realm of the everyday. Imagine what you could do to show off a collection of vintage mixing bowls! Establishing sense of depth is key. Combine two- and three-dimensional pieces. When creating a vignette that includes a surface like a mantel or a tabletop, mix objects of varying heights.

Furnishings and art objects always reveal their beauty within an environment, like gems in a setting. They work in concert with the colors chosen for walls, trim, and ceiling, the surrounding materials and textures, the shape of the space, and the prevailing light. A whole host of visual considerations accompanies a handful of objects.

As you craft vignettes in your own home, take photographs throughout the process to help you evaluate your space with clear eyes. This is particularly helpful when you have lived in a home long enough to lose sight of its features and quirks. You may be surprised to find that the unadorned windows you like so well are making the room look extremely stark. Perhaps your velvet sofa looks more mousy than luxurious because there isn't enough contrast between it and the color of the wall.

If you feel something is lacking or out of balance in your budding vignette, keep a photo to guide you until you find the elusive detail that will tie it together. When you are satisfied at last, you may be delighted to discover that your photo would look right at home in the pages of a design book or magazine. Of course, no matter how wonderful the photo, the greatest reward for your efforts will be living in and enjoying your own artful home.

A casual, modern sensibility animates a vignette laden with traditional glamour. With only four carefully considered elements—table, chair, vase, and artwork—the arrangement flaunts the exquisite grain of the dark wood furnishings against an elegant neutral color palette. Ruthless editing is the key. Picture the console table covered end to end with knickknacks. Surely you'd still notice its beautiful lyre-shaped base, but the complexity of its wood grain might not command the same attention.

No Mere **Seat**

Everybody has quirks, from hidden depths of feeling to unexpected outbursts of wit. As we move through the world, our personalities reveal themselves in gestures large and small. The places we live, on the other hand, are not always so distinctive. Some rooms are boxy and featureless, defined strictly by rectangles and right angles. Other rooms are filled with furnishings and accessories that perfectly reflect the decorating crazes of the moment, but confide very little about the inhabitant's true passions.

When you bring artwork into your home, your own personality bubbles up to the surface. Just one imaginative, well-crafted piece can make an indelible mark on the space. Consider this distinctive chair at the left forged by sister-and-brother blacksmiths. No mere seat, it is a magical landscape dotted with dogwood blossoms. The artists have used the ancient tradition of metalsmithing to pay tribute to beauty in the natural world.

Is this chair practical? Probably not, if you need a matched set of six or eight for your dining room.

Is this chair an extravagance? Some might think so. It certainly would be wasted if cast in the minor role of one-of-many living room chairs. Like any complicated, multi-layered character, this memorable chair can carry a lot more weight and meaning than that.

Is this chair valuable? Yes, incalculably, if it embodies ideas you hold dear, provides enduring satisfaction, and reveals a tiny bit about what makes your heart beat faster.

Be offbeat in your approach. For this entryway, a playful chair looks refreshingly different with a mélange of flowers, objects, and art to welcome guests into the home.

just *a thought*

In 1913, Elsie de Wolfe, who is credited with singlehandedly inventing the profession of interior design, wrote *The House in Good Taste*. In this seminal book she boldly declared, "I know of nothing more significant than the awakening of men and women throughout our country to the desire to improve their houses."

That's what I have—the desire to improve my house, over and over again! I am a serial redecorator, and sometimes a new acquisition is all it takes to get me started. For instance, I recently purchased a terrific lamp, which led to new paint in my living room (I always wanted an orange room) and rearrangement of all the paintings in the house. Suddenly, my world feels fresh and different.

My home is an evolving landscape of my changing tastes and interests; it's a many-colored reflection of my life. Today, I pause to appreciate all that I have accomplished, trusting that tomorrow will bring new ideas for improvement.

Twenty squares, rich in color, texture, and pattern, encode one family's story—this artist works with clients to create what she calls "memory tapestries." Surrounding details like flowers, pears, and pillows pick up on this focal point's visual cues.

Finding a Focal Point

One commanding piece can set the mood for an entire room, bring color to an unadorned wall, or reshape a space. Perhaps a fabulous object catches your eye, compelling you to find a perfect home for it. Or perhaps the very uniqueness of a space inspires you to complete it with something equally special. Think of the curved wall of a turret room, a fifteen-foot expanse in a great room, a bare spot between two imposing windows, or the underused space on a landing.

Many suitable possibilities leap to mind—a sculpture, a painting of generous proportions, an impressive piece of glass. But you'll find it rewarding to consider less conventional options as well—a swath of sumptuous textiles, a remarkable piece of furniture, a group of ceramic tiles displayed as a single work of art.

Whatever you choose to display, make sure the artwork doesn't have to compete with its surroundings for attention. This is not to say that your walls must be stark white—a dramatic color contrast can be quite striking—but the artwork shouldn't have to jockey for visual real estate with nearby pieces. Think of an art gallery, where the work takes center stage and holds its viewer's imagination in its grip. The wise curator allows each piece ample breathing room, so that the undistracted viewer fully experiences the artist's vision.

Your chosen focal point may be the most striking element in a room, but don't lose sight of the whole composition. Look for ways to establish subtle harmonies between the focal point and its surroundings. For example, if you are highlighting a fiber wall hanging, consider upholstering a chair in the room with cloth of a similar texture. Or introduce accents like a few well-placed throw pillows or candles to echo a beautiful color in a piece.

Shown here above a fireplace, this sculptural wall piece is a perfect example of an unusual focal point. Although made of paper, it resembles monumental pieces of striated rock.

The drawing in this hallway is large, but not unusually so. Instead, the powerful impact of scaling up derives from the size of the heads depicted and the tension of their relationship within the frame.

Playing with Scale

Today, we live in homes that are bigger than ever. Do those extra square feet and vaulted ceilings expand our possibilities for enchantment? They certainly can, when we make room for artwork and furnishings that restore our sense of wonder and play.

The best of rooms contain elements of self-assertion and attitude, the exuberance of a personality revealed. Scaling up is an engaging way to create visual interest and underscore emotional significance. Things we are accustomed to seeing small become intriguing—even magical—when re-imagined at a much larger size.

If your home has ample space for the imagination to roam, try adding drama and fun with works of art that are larger than life. Remember when you were small? Seen through young eyes, every color blazed brighter and the furniture cast extra-long shadows. Those days may be gone, but in the hands of artists, everyday objects can regain a touch of the fantastic.

A trio of enormous wooden vessels tells a story of contrasting textures.

Rising up toward sixteen-foot-high ceilings, a benevolent angel stands guard over the bed, almost sharing the sky with the world outside. The photograph was reproduced on canvas rather than photo paper to create a much larger print.

Adding Texture and Material

The word *texture* derives from a Latin word meaning to weave. It works on multiple levels, referring both to the surface characteristics of an object and to the less apparent ways that structure emerges from a gathering of individual threads.

Each material or medium possesses its own essential character. Fiber and wood are warm and nurturing, while glass is clean, utilitarian, and a platform for color. Stone is strong and stable. Metal is cool and decorative. Clay is earthy and elemental. Within each category, however, each material can display infinite nuances of texture. Wood can be varnished to a high gloss or left unsanded. Glass can be pocked and cloudy or crystal clear.

The rooms or vignettes in your home are compositions where furnishings, artwork, and other objects complement, connect with, even converse with each other. Compelling textural relationships can make the difference between rooms that merely match and rooms that have depth and soul.

Like a color, a certain type of texture can dominate or work as an accent. Consider big wooden bowls, chunky baskets, or curvy stoneware vessels—all rather rough hewn. Put them in a similarly rugged setting, complete with wide-plank floors, furniture with weathered painted finishes, and couches clad in canvas slipcovers, and you'll have a laid-back and comfortable living room.

Stone walls set the stage for interplay between textures rough and smooth. Glass and satin-finished wood contrast with scooped carving and lavish layers of silk, while a harmonious autumnal palette deepens the richness of the arrangement.

Now picture the same pieces in a room defined by terrazzo floors and clean-lined furnishings. A few handmade, organic touches, all from the same texture family, quickly warm up a cool, contemporary space.

Sumptuous textural contrasts dress up monochromatic color palettes. Think white-on-white or, perhaps, shades of beige. There is more to luxury than meets the eye: texture and feel are usually the key. Glossy lacquer, nubby linen, embroidered cotton, softest cashmere knit, supple leather, matte stone—when color takes a step back, you can combine all of these materials with abandon. Well suited to bedrooms or spa-style bathrooms, the low-color, high-texture approach results in exceptionally restful settings.

Of all places in the home, the table begs for texture. Here, a woven mat and dried branches make natural companions for glazed ceramic pieces embellished with coils and freeform incisions.

A glossy tiled floor lays the groundwork for a study in geometry. Two columns of black squares in the stained glass door echo the floor tiles. Overlapping shapes—circles, triangles, and rectangles—and touches of color establish a dynamic counterpoint for the rigorous grids of black or transparent squares.

Appreciating Geometry

Some days we race distractedly through streets and shopping malls pulsing with color, light, and noise. We arrive home only to be swept away once more on a rising tide of media. Television and movies to watch, magazines to flip through, websites to surf. In our cluttered culture, the goal of keeping things simple seems unattainable.

Perhaps a return to square roots is in order. Art and design inspired by basic geometry can help restore our focus on essentials. Purity of line, color, and shape bring homes—and lives—into balance.

Living with abstract artwork, particularly geometrically abstract artwork, clears the mind and places interpretation squarely in the eye of the beholder. Contemplating an abstract piece offers a refreshing respite from digesting predetermined narratives or experiencing pressure to do, feel, or buy certain things. In the modern world, demands on our attention are frequent and forceful. Our senses are under constant assault. But at home, surrounded by enough space to breathe, bold colors and shapes can add welcome clarity. The secret is making artful choices about what to live with and editing out the rest. Whether you are an artist or not, this is one line you can draw.

Lattice screens mark the entrance to this living room with formal symmetry. Inside, the room splits into two equal parts along an axis defined by the coffee table and fireplace. Above, a tray ceiling picks up the rhythm of the stepped fireplace surround. Although geometry and symmetry are guiding principles behind this design, it also possesses considerable warmth and softness, thanks to a pastel palette, sheer balloon shades, and glass etched with delicate flowers.

The Character of Color

As a manifestation of light and energy, color holds the power to soothe or stimulate. It is the single most important element in creating an appealing environment.

Thoughtful color choices support and strengthen your sense of style. Do you crave the energy generated by strong contrasts, or would you rather relax, surrounded by a range of subtle shades? If you are not sure what suits you, look through pictures in books and magazines or take cues from combinations found in nature. Learn to recognize different color schemes and how they work together. Complementary pairings bounce opposites off one another. Monochromatic palettes layer many permutations of a single hue. Analogous palettes feature several colors that sit side by side on the color wheel—red, orange and yellow, for example, or yellow, green, blue.

Works of art, especially paintings, prints, and glass, are ideal vehicles for color in your home. Trust the artist's eye and imagination to come up with exciting combinations you would never think of putting together. Consider using the hues of a favorite object as a springboard for an entire room's design.

As you cultivate your personal palette, think about the way light moves through each room as the days and seasons pass. To a certain degree, your location—near the ocean or the desert, in a city of glass and concrete, or amid green fields—will dictate the intensity and path of light and, thereby, the character of color in your home.

cultivate your personal palette

Living in Color

Small amounts of hot color ignite this contemporary bedroom. Sculpture and bedding stand out against a canvas of white carpet, walls, and furnishings. Used liberally, neutrals—like the white that dominates here—provide a foundation for full-strength doses of color.

Play with colors that pack a lot of punch. Your home can handle it. The warm hug of chocolate brown. Yellow's bright smile. Lime green's mischievous wink. The kiss of pink. Each color has a distinctive personality and its own way of welcoming you into a room.

If you have an open floor plan, it's all too easy to paint everything with the least obtrusive denominator. Instead, plan areas of strong color that will sculpt and define the space. For example, if the kitchen flows right into the dining area, try flooding the kitchen with a light, cheerful color and choosing a warm and inviting dark color that will foster intimacy in the dining area.

Cool teal and butter yellow stripes on the wall set the tone for a harmonious vignette.
The painted decoration on the table picks up colors in the print. The porcelain vessel
adds texture with its ribbed surface and spiky sea-urchin top.

A single colorful accent wall can transform a room. Think about how you can use color to showcase an architectural focal point or bring out the best in a favorite piece of furniture. A backdrop of color makes a beautiful frame for a fireplace, dining room buffet, or unusual headboard. Keep the effect simple and sophisticated by using a deeper shade of the room's dominant color. Or choose a contrasting color for a striking, contemporary look.

With so many fabulous colors available, you wonder, how on earth do I choose? Look for inspiration in things you already love, and you won't find yourself at the mercy of the next spin of the color forecaster's wheel. One rug, print, or painting could hold enough variety to inspire a palette for your entire home. Single out hues you like and let a different one dominate in each room. Rely on hardwood flooring or a shared trim color to establish common threads throughout the home.

The color spectrum presents an infinitely varied cast of characters. Go ahead and give a few of them starring roles on the stage of your home.

White ceilings and trim work bridge two strong wall colors, defining a casual dining area that is crisp and fresh, without feeling confrontational. With so much structural drama, a limited number of carefully edited accents completes the space.

just *a thought*

My personal definition of hell is a world of all black and white. That's why I especially love the jewel tones and exuberant colors of contemporary glass artists. When I come across glass objects dressed in brilliant reds, yellows, and blues, I want to take them home and redecorate my living room!

Blown glass has a rich heritage that goes back 2,000 years. Today's glass artists combine ancient methods with new ideas and aesthetics. The glass vessel has become the canvas on which the artist expresses ideas about balance, space, light, and color.

Alive to all the possibilities of color, artists give us beautiful glass forms that take the breath away. Don't leave color to the flowers in your garden. Instead, open your home to objects that express your individuality—vividly.

A surprising hue for a bookcase, ocean blue looks even more striking against deep orange—its complement on the color wheel.

Decorative accents present wonderful opportunities for waking up living spaces with bright color. Switch pieces out seasonally to keep the look fresh.

In this sunny dining room, three contrasting colors of window trim share a common source in a custom-painted floorcloth.

The clean, simple lines of modern furniture are visually pronounced in white environments. A collection of small black-and-white photographs works nicely against the white wall without overpowering the space.

Exploring Color: A Primer

Learning how colors behave in their relationships with each other, with ambient light, and with different materials and textures takes time and requires willingness to experiment. Each color carries enduring cultural associations and elicits strong emotional—and even physical—responses. Colors also possess properties of warmth or coolness that are forceful enough to temper the effects of light or shape spatial perceptions. Generally speaking, warm colors such as red, orange, and yellow press forward; cool colors such as green, blue, and violet recede.

The saturated primary, secondary, and tertiary hues around a color wheel can take off in any number of directions. Add white to achieve tints of lighter value. Add black or a color's complement (its opposite on the color wheel) to produce shades of darker value.

White

The paradox of pure, innocent white is that its lack of color *is* its color. This makes it the traditional choice as a background, so that everything around it stands out in contrast. Be attentive to the many shades of white; by adding touches of other colors, you can achieve just the right blend to balance the brightness with feelings of warmth and comfort.

Black

Black creates a sense of intrigue and depth. If applied sparingly, it can be used as an elegant background to highlight framed works of art and set off other colors. For some, its mystery can be magical and sexy, while for others, too much black feels somber and uncomfortable.

Gray

Hovering somewhere between black and white, gray has become a fashionable background color. It reflects a modern aesthetic and works well in combination with other colors. Pale shades of gray, such as pearl gray, are very effective in setting off bold and colorful framed art.

Brown

Brown connects us to our roots. Lighter shades of brown, like beige, tan, and sand, create an earthy feel, while darker shades can feel murky and foreboding in large doses. Mixed with shades of red, brown absorbs glare and softens the impact of the sun in environments where the light is harsh and the climate is dry.

Red

A color of power and passion, true red is best applied sparingly, as a dramatic accent. Try red in combination with blues, greens, and yellows when you want a vibrant pop. If you'd like to cover a larger area, earthier shades like terra cotta and coral are pleasing choices. Deep, dark burgundy reds make excellent complements to dark woods in formal rooms.

Pink

Feminine and nurturing, pink is known to have soothing qualities. It's a favorite hue for bedrooms and children's rooms, where it creates a sense of softness and calm.

Orange

Vibrant orange is often associated with health and wellness. Earthy orange tones have become popular accents, especially in areas where the light is misty and the climate is damp. Orange represents optimism and adds a welcoming note to entryways and hallways. It tends to brighten a space, stimulating conversation and ideas.

An artful home environment can be confined to an area as small as one's sofa. Here, bright orange pops against a neutral couch, adding playfulness and energy to an otherwise ordinary seat.

Large areas of bright yellow can be overwhelming without places for the eye to stop and rest. A pair of black sweeping wall sconces draws the eye to a tulip-themed vignette in contrasting colors.

Yellow

This is a color that's all about energy. Yellow represents the power of the sun and is associated with vitality, intellect, and longevity. Pale, warm shades of yellow, like lemon, are becoming fashionable in dining rooms, where friends and family gather. Darker shades, like saffron and sunflower, are attractive accent colors on doors and window trim.

Green

Green is the color of nature and growth. It's at the center of the color spectrum and stimulates feelings of harmony and peace. Green is a color of balance; it is highly adaptable and its restful properties make it ideal for use in lighter shades as a neutral or background color. Darker shades like moss or forest absorb glare beautifully.

Blue

Blue is associated with introspection, tranquility, and serenity. It also represents the spirit and energy of water. Blue induces sleep and lighter shades, like sky blue, are favorites for use in bedrooms. If you are drawn to blue, study the way the entire blue spectrum is used in Scandinavia, a region of long, dark winters and sparkling, bright summers.

Purple

Regal purple is considered an artistic color and is associated with meditation, ritual, and spirituality. Darker shades, like plum, include more red and are thus associated with fire and passion. Lighter shades, like lavender and soft violet, promote a lovely, subtle sense of solitude and reflection in a bedroom, den, or library.

A classical gold mosaic shines in a field of complementary green tiles, eliciting feelings of peace and renewal. Clear glass doors ensure soothing sensations beyond the confines of the shower.

Reinforce a theme with color. A curled ceramic swimmer and a calm ocean view invite the viewer to dive in to this serene scene. The bold blue wall further emphasizes themes of sky and sea.

just *a thought*

For as long as I can remember, purple has been my favorite color. Just ask my poor mother, who suffered through my high school years with the purple bedroom walls, bedspread, and curtains, along with clothing in various shades of purple or plum and the all-important lavender senior prom dress.

Over the years, my aesthetic preferences have matured and changed. With maturity comes new color discoveries. Nothing serene and sedate, mind you! These days, I love rich colors that grab your attention and make you smile with joy.

Introduce color in surprising spots—a geranium red coffee table or a delphinium blue lamp. An unexpected jolt of color can give the whole room depth and energy. Even small objects infused with color will influence the feel of a room.

These spots of color brighten my home and my spirit. My friend Bobbie calls it color therapy. Personally, I look to my home to provide not just space to live in, but also space for my imagination to roam.

And I still love purple.

The Art of White Walls

While color can change everything with a few daring strokes of the brush, sometimes painting walls white is the most confident and expressive choice of all.

When color takes a back seat, the subtler textures of your materials come into focus. Frosted glass, crinkled silk, intricate brocade, velvet, rough canvas, marble, glossy paint—it's easier to appreciate the depth and variety of the surfaces in a room when the overarching color is constant and neutral.

Other compositional elements that come to the forefront in a white room are the shapes of the objects within it. The graceful curve of a table leg, the shadow cast by a wrought-iron chair, the stark angularity of a minimalist sculpture—these details are all the more poignant or arresting when the simplicity of their surroundings allows them to shine.

Overstuffed white furnishings disappear against white walls, putting the focus squarely on intricately textured objects and vibrant works of art.

White walls showcase this homeowner's collection of contemporary art and craft. Iridescent blue tiles around the fireplace contribute a splash of cool color at the heart of the room.

With a white theme, it's easy to switch out colorful accents seasonally. Even if you keep larger pieces like furnishings and rugs in place throughout the year, small adjustments could have a big impact on the mood of the room. For example, summery green apples and bright flowers might give way to earthier notes like a basket of pinecones or heaps of river stones in the fall.

There is a simple reason why so many galleries have white walls and so many fine restaurants serve food on white plates: A neutral background allows the artists' or chefs' creations to reveal themselves more purely and more fully. Likewise, white rooms in our homes let the nuances of our personalities stand out in vivid relief.

Living *with* Beautiful Objects

The urge to gather, display, and collect objects lies very deep in the human psyche. Most of us select or choose to keep the objects we live with because they have a special meaning, such as the wooden bowl purchased on a trip or the piece of pottery received as a birthday gift from a sister. Sometimes, at a craft fair or flea market, a certain piece reaches out and grabs the heart, demanding to be taken home.

Many of us seek out the unusual, the original, and the handmade. Objects made by artists are much more than eye candy; they speak to us and move us. They tell stories. We take them home, learn their stories by heart, and add our personal embellishments along the way.

When seeking a new piece of artwork, look carefully at the object's shape, note the materials it was made from, and investigate the artist who made it. Purchase with conviction. This is an object that you will live with for a long time; it will influence your mood every time you look at it and make a statement about who you are.

But, most importantly, live with what you love, collect what you crave, and present it with confidence. In the next two chapters, I'll share ideas for incorporating art into your everyday life. I'll begin with small objects to create atmosphere and mood, and then proceed to artwork for walls and floors.

live with what you love

Dressing Your Home's Intimate Spaces

Each three-dimensional place in your home—from nooks and crannies to open staircases and entryways—presents an opportunity to showcase objects in the round. Our treasured objects contribute color, texture, and form, and define the space that surrounds them with sensuous curves or sharp angles—or something in between. Large or small, functional or non-functional, objects are essential elements for adorning and embellishing our homes. Here, then, are a few categories of objets d'art to consider.

Sculpture

Cast or carved, for floor or tabletop, sculpture represents a commitment to a form of expression dating back to prehistoric times, and later made famous by the likes of Michelangelo and Donatello. Typically created as one-of-a-kind pieces or in limited editions, today's sculptures may depict forms from our world or express abstract or architectural ideas. A large sculpture's sheer presence and craftsmanship is impressive, while small sculpture amazes with its attention to detail, calling for a more intimate examination. Sculpture fashioned from found objects puts a new, environmentally friendly spin on an age-old tradition.

As the centerpiece for the dining room table, this organic glass sculpture brings an element of the home's visible garden front and center. No fresh flowers required!

Vessels

The vessel, our earliest art form, remains the vital heart of the fine craft world. This is the form that ceramic, glass, metal, basket, and wood artists return to again and again. Open container forms, whether tall cylindrical vessels or low spreading bowls, carry a memory of all the pots of civilization. The best vessels take on an individual identity and contribute to the tradition.

Lamps and Lighting

Contemporary artists are pushing boundaries with innovative lighting designed to elevate and illuminate the spaces in which we live, work, and play. Expertly crafted in every medium, these lamps, sconces, and chandeliers reflect every style—from traditional to playful to ultramodern—in a wide range of prices. Multiple lighting elements can artfully unite a home's disparate spaces, affecting our moods and daily experiences in a way no other medium can.

On or off, this hanging lamp is an exciting force in its environment. Not only does it light a room beautifully, it also says something about its owner's character and style.

Some vessels are quiet and functional; others say more about form and less about function. At times the function is no function at all, other than providing a beautiful visual experience.

Always check with the artist or gallery before you assume your tabletop piece is food, oven, microwave, or dishwasher safe. Some functional objects may require special care or instructions.

Functional Objects

The coffee mug made by a local ceramist. The handmade wooden clock you found at the antique shop. The blown glass goblets you fell in love with at an artist's studio. These functional works of art appeal especially to our sense of touch and remind us with each use of a special person, time, or place. They link up with our habits, and we rely on them to add artful character to our daily routines and special occasions. Functional objects are fertile ground for collections, as they are often produced in larger editions, in wildly varying mediums and styles.

Decorative Objects

There's no limit to what can be deemed an artful object. Pillows, books, boxes, candles, and even small trinkets can all be artful if you choose. Position your object in a place of honor, such as on the mantel or on the dining room table, to call attention to its creative purpose. Group like or unlike objects together as a unique collection. Arrange objects in relation to paintings or prints of a similar theme, color scheme, or shape to wed wall to floor or tabletop. No matter how it was made in the first place, an object is primarily what you make of it.

This contemporary bronze sculpture of a reclining nude is perfectly at home with four ivory button clasps from Namibia (displayed here as sculptural objects), and a small stack of coffee-table books.

just *a thought*

The objects of my life are a form of autobiography. They are tangible evidence of places I've lived, relationships I've had, travels made, and occasions celebrated.

I wander around my home and note the idiosyncratic blend of art and objects, and it is a reflection on the unfolding of my life. There are pieces of folk pottery that I began collecting in college. And there is the large painting I purchased after college, when I was so broke that it was paid off in monthly installments to the gallery.

Other mementos include prizes found while traveling (Chinese pottery and Japanese lacquerware) and special gifts from friends and family. The sculpture given to me as a wedding gift by my mentor so many years ago is a daily reminder of the lessons learned from this wonderful man, even though he's been gone for a long time now.

When we celebrated our twentieth wedding anniversary, my husband and I decided to commemorate this important occasion with a special gift to one another: a Bennett Bean ceramic vessel. We feel that Bennett's work shines with a richness and joy that symbolizes our relationship. This piece now occupies a place of honor in our home and hearts.

Decorating Creatively

In a home where objects take center stage, you are the director and executive producer. In your arrangements of art and objects, you are able to unleash your imagination and create personal still lifes with the things you love.

Designer George Nelson, one of the most inventive minds of the twentieth century, described creativity as "the sudden realization that one has taken a lot of disconnected pieces and found…a way of putting them together."

This is your opportunity to think out of the box. Pair objects nonchalantly with paintings. Trust your instincts, and put all of your artwork with a common color theme together on a series of shelves. With practice, chutzpah, and a little luck, insights are gained and wonderful things happen.

The true creative act produces something that never existed before. Paint a section of the wall behind an object a different tone than the rest of the room so that the shape and texture of the piece are thrown into relief. Ceramic plates picked up at a flea market look great mounted on a wall painted a deep color.

At 21 inches high x 30 inches wide (53 x 76 cm), this metal sculpture makes a beautiful impression on a living room mantel when framed by the light yellow paint on the wall behind. Alternately, it could prove a wonderful contemporary contrast when placed on a traditional fireplace hearth.

just *a thought*

Some people paint, some people sculpt. I arrange. And rearrange. And rearrange once again.

It starts when I acquire a new, very special piece. Like the ceramic teapot that serves tea perfectly well, but really wants to live on the shelf next to the basket and the turned wood bowl. (Not only do these objects seem to have a relationship, but I'm convinced that they talk with one another when the lights go out at night.)

Suddenly, I find myself taking everything off all my shelves, re-creating a home for my objects that feels fresh and different. Providing a clean slate for my imagination helps me see the things I love in new ways. To my delight, I sometimes discover different forms of presentation. Did you know that it is perfectly acceptable to put pottery on top of a pile of books? By the way, my favorite small photograph looks beautiful beside the new teapot.

Even though my husband sighs when he sees that I am on a rearranging binge once again, he understands that the shelves are my canvas, a place for expressing my creativity with the things that I love.

Combine things that don't strictly go together. Cool and warm colors can be arranged in balanced compositions, creating a rich vignette. For a measure of surprise, pair contemporary pieces with antiques. Qualities like color, texture, and size are all variable elements of the mix. Your creative displays should be full of attitude and independence, intelligence and wit—a heavenly abundance of beautiful things.

And, the most important lesson about creative decorating (to say nothing of life): If it doesn't make you happy, change it. Life is short!

A clean-lined gilt frame forges harmonious relationships with both the gold tones in the painting and the handsome form of the dresser. An uncluttered surface highlights the pleasing shape of a flat box that would be easy to miss in a busier setting.

Establishing
Relationships

Works of art are, in their own way, as responsive to their immediate environment as people are. That is why it is helpful to be sensitive to the way objects respond to one another in a room setting.

But don't worry! If you buy pieces you truly love, they will all go together. It's like having a great dinner party. Some pieces are loud and brash, others quiet and restrained. Everyone will end up friends, bound together by your own personal affection.

Collections of ceramics, glass, turned wood, or whatever happens to be your particular passion, have an aesthetic as well as intrinsic value. Introduce them to one another in a single area, where they can make a strong decorative statement. Line up a selection of small pitchers, and watch them march across the top of your desk. Bring out all of the antique purses that you have picked up here and there over the years, and group them together on a wall.

If you have a particularly important object, study its form and structure. Rather than placing it in a crowded arrangement, imagine how it will look with enough space around it so that it can breathe. Let it interact with the painting overhead, which can serve the purpose of framing the object and focusing the eye.

Remember, a personal collection of objects doesn't have to be expensive to be eye-worthy. Sometimes the most ordinary pieces, imaginatively displayed, can be more fun to look at than a cabinet full of cut crystal. All you need are empty shelves or a blank wall, a good sense of arrangement, and the courage to be creative.

Despite their varied style and subject matter, a collection of small wall hangings works together when framed in similar simple frames. Likewise, a row of similarly sized vessels and art objects provide pleasing verticality to the desk's strong horizontal lines. Wall pieces and objects share a similar color palette, completing this charming workspace.

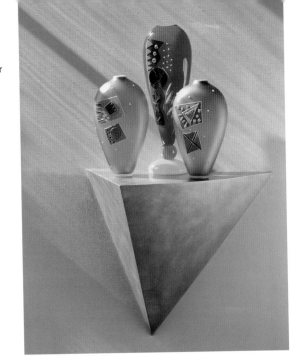

Think color and material when choosing shelves for your artful objects. This steel wall shelf complements bright glass vessels while blending perfectly into the wall behind, giving the objects the appearance of floating.

Opportunities for Display

Objects here, objects there, objects everywhere. Where can you put all of these objects of desire? You should view every tabletop, and any other flat surface in your home, as an opportunity to display beautiful and interesting things that contribute to telling your personal story.

Shelves

Shelves provide support without being noticed; they serve their function admirably without distracting from your artwork. Whether wall-mounted or built-in, they are an ideal method of displaying all sorts of objects. Intersperse books and artwork for visual interest, or place books flat with a piece on top for a refreshing change.

Consoles and Hall Tables

Consoles and hall tables serve as the workhorses of the display world. Their horizontal surfaces allow for groupings of large and small art objects, as well as books, flowers, and candlesticks. Objects can be placed informally, as if by chance, or arranged symmetrically to create a more formal look. The color of the background wall and the artwork hanging above the table complete the perfect arrangement.

Large antique vessels sitting atop this classic wood hall table serve as visual bookends to the abstract painting above in an unexpected yet compatible combination of artistic styles.

Coffee Tables

Coffee tables are the gathering place of the living room and, as such, provide a natural spot to place prized pieces. Your guests are quite close to these objects, so artwork with pattern and intricate details of handwork can be particularly effective.

Consider your coffee table to be a stage on which you arrange objects in the "theater" of your room. The incongruous trio of objects on this artist-made coffee table mimics the colors and patterns of the art print and sofa pillow behind.

Precise and moody, the painting above this little chest provides an intriguing backdrop to a group of art objects, books, and antiques, calling the visitor in for a more intimate inspection of the homeowner's personal treasures.

A large painting is beautifully displayed in an architectural niche that provides an appropriate viewing environment for a vibrant work that needs its own space to breathe.

Chests and Side Tables

Chests and side tables provide the perfect stage for small vignettes. Mix unrelated but compatible objects for some diversity. Try a collection of smooth stones (so nice to the touch!) or a pair of tall silver candlesticks to help you define a more horizontal or vertical display.

Alcoves and Niches

An alcove is visible on a floor plan: it bumps out a room's perimeter, although its ceiling may be lower than the room's ceiling. A niche is set into a wall, somewhere above floor level. Either of these recessed spaces provides a dramatic setting for special objects that are valuable and need protection. Negative space frames the pieces housed within and creates instant visual impact.

Alcoves and niches are often painted the same color as the surrounding walls, but painting the inside a dark or bright color is a stunning way to highlight objects on display. Install overhead lighting to heighten the drama.

Primary colors blue and red contrast starkly in this combined wall niche/alcove, perfect for focusing the eye on just a few striking pieces.

Windowsills

Windowsills are particularly well suited to anything that needs backlighting, such as pots of flowers. This is an ideal location for glass pieces, as strong natural light brings out the brilliant colors.

Floor

The floor is an overlooked display surface, providing for three-dimensional viewing of interesting pieces of artwork. Large, heavy pieces are obvious candidates for floor display, but consider stacking piles of antique suitcases, or grouping taller candlesticks in corners, staircase landings, or other unobtrusive spaces.

Glass, metal, and ceramic objects are good choices for windowsills as their colors are impervious to sunlight (and are, in fact, usually enhanced by it).

Positioned against the wall in a low-traffic area, this print provides a surprising visual delight, particularly to those seated on the couch.

The bronze sculpture on the steel pedestal in the foreground is given a place of honor in this home while visually balanced with a small collection of sculptures by the same artist, shown behind.

Pedestals

Often works of art in their own right, pedestals are a classic choice for showcasing single objects, particularly sculpture or a vessel that is best appreciated from all sides. Pedestals serve an important purpose by placing these valued objects closer to eye level, so viewers can see and admire their details. Consider using a pedestal with interior illumination to bring out the spectacular colors of art glass.

Lighting *Artwork and Objects*

Making artwork the focus of your home involves more than just finding a suitable place to put it. Carefully considered accent lighting gives your favorite pieces a chance to shine.

Showcasing three-dimensional artwork generally requires light that is several times brighter and more focused than the ambient lighting in a room. Of course, different types of artwork lead to different lighting solutions.

- Try installing strip lighting on bookshelves or in cabinets to emphasize the forms and textures of objects assembled there. This is an excellent way to display a collection of ceramics, but you could highlight anything from small paintings to woven baskets or inlaid wooden boxes in this manner.

- It is most effective to light sculpture or art glass from multiple positions. For example, two ceiling-mounted spotlights trained on opposite sides of a piece will illuminate its contours beautifully. Before installing elegant, but expensive, recessed lighting, strategize with clip-on spotlights or flashlights to identify the optimum combination of light sources.

- Sections of track lighting with adjustable halogen bulbs are the most flexible and cost-effective option for lighting a mixture of two- and three-dimensional objects in a room. Be aware that intense light can generate enough heat to damage fragile materials. To prevent this, pay attention to lighting product specifications and install the light source at a sufficient distance from the artwork.

Are treasured works of art languishing in the shadows of your home? Thoughtful accent lighting can signal the importance of these pieces to you and invite the attention and admiration they deserve.

A joyful, sophisticated atmosphere permeates this living room, thanks to well-placed lighting. Down lighting illuminates the tablescapes. Also beautifully lit from above is the statue of Quan Yin, an Asian goddess. A traditional Japanese vessel and art glass are safely and beautifully displayed in lighted art niches.

Displaying Small Treasures

One small object is nice, and a grouping of small objects is even nicer. Special treasures need to be treated with the respect they deserve.

Placing a group of objects on a tray, or lining pieces up across the top of a desk or shelf, adds significance to the display. Often, it helps to visually frame a piece, either by using a small picture frame (for that crocheted handkerchief from your grandmother) or by locating it on a small shelf (for the antique bottle that is light green in the sunlight).

If you have a charming piece, let it make friends with the furniture. Vases and candlesticks can be admired at conversational level when assembled together on a coffee table. Tabletops are excellent display points for smaller objects that need to be viewed in the round.

If you love the work of a particular artist, try grouping his or her work together in a collection. Though various colors are highlighted in this playful ceramic collection, the similarity of style clearly links the pieces to the same artist.

just *a thought*

I am a lamp freak. My collection includes beautiful and exotic lamps made by artist-friends, as well as unusual pieces (I say "unusual," my husband says "strange") found in flea markets. All serve to shed light on my activities and inactivities, transform the rooms of my home, and occasionally, transform my life.

These purposes are far too important to leave to the pedestrian lamps found in department stores. My lamps serve as beacons. They illuminate my surroundings and brighten my moods. They shape my view of the world.

The object lesson taught by the artists working with lighting is that function can be—should be—an artful blend of utility and beauty. It is not enough that the objects we use do the things they are intended to do. Lamps should grace the spaces they occupy and have some character as well. Artful lamps radiate presence as well as light.

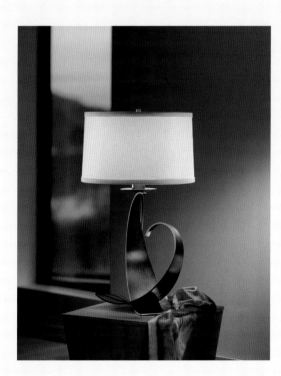

A large, eye-catching sculpture can serve as a wonderful icebreaker when guests enter your home; every piece you purchase has a story behind it.

Adding
a Showstopper

A single large object, prominently displayed, can be the showstopper of any room. The display for this kind of piece needs a generous amount of space and lighting to achieve full impact.

One superb piece, placed in an entryway, welcomes visitors. A plain display stand or pedestal can play a supporting role to a sculpture or vessel. Make sure the room is spacious enough to display the object without it becoming an obstruction.

The objects you select to feature in your home speak volumes about you, your taste, and your style. Let your imagination loose and consider the possibilities: a large, striking photograph or mirror propped on a side table; a piece of pottery filled with tall dried flowers placed on a table in the center of a room; or a vertical ceramic wall sculpture hung over the fireplace. With one showstopping piece of artwork, a simple display can bring focus and excitement to any room.

Large, colorless walls benefit from a grand piece of artwork. Think about how you can breathe life onto boxy spaces with texture, color, and curve.

Hung at varying distances from the wall, these fiber-wrapped wall sculptures provide color, texture, and undulating depth to an otherwise flat space. Relief sculpture has the potential to cast interesting and ever-changing shadows, adding to its artistic value.

Decorating
Walls *and* Floors

Walls and floors present the homeowner's greatest challenge: What to do with those large blank spaces?

In selecting what will reside on our walls and floors, we can choose any medium—or a mixture of media. Challenge gives way to opportunity, thanks to the photographers, printmakers, weavers, glassmakers, ceramicists, papermakers, and woodworkers—the artists who sculpt and paint in every imaginable medium.

Choose paintings, prints, and photographs to bring walls to life. Some tell stories or honor the people and places that are important to you. Others, more abstract, set imaginations in motion or create moods with color. Take risks with two-dimensional artwork—this is your chance to set functional concerns aside and focus on how a work of art makes you feel.

On the other hand, practical needs often trump emotional ones when it comes to the floors of your home. If comfort is your primary consideration, look to natural materials that will warm and soften cold surfaces and, more importantly, delight bare feet.

In the artful home, each wall, floor, or ceiling, for that matter, is a canvas for creativity, a promising composition in its own right. With so many beautiful, inventive things to hang, lay flat, or build right into surfaces, our palettes are full indeed.

a canvas for creativity

Bringing Walls to Life

The works of art on your walls are windows to the soul—your soul, and the souls of the artists who created them. Each type of artwork possesses certain characteristics, and I will discuss some of those qualities. I will also look beyond the artist's immediate field of vision and address external details such as choosing frames and wall colors and arranging multiple elements.

Paintings and Drawings

Paintings and drawings are one of a kind. No matter what the style or subject matter, this is their essential attribute and the key to their value. Once complete, each claims an utterly unique space in the world. Consequently, the decision to share your home with such a singular creation is a deeply intimate one. Most art dealers counsel their patrons, above all, to buy what captivates them. A compelling work of art says something important and true about the artist who made it as well as the person who chose it. With each look, it will reveal something new.

Built-in cabinetry displaying a variety of artist-made objects creates a beautiful frame for this oil painting.

Surrounded by books, this painting opens up a wonderful vista on a windowless wall. The gold leaf on the wood frame is elegant and narrow—it doesn't distract from the expansive view.

Prints

Often confused with reproductions, which are mere copies of works of art, prints are artworks in and of themselves. Each print is a unique impression of an original artwork that is reproduced in multiple. The complete body of multiple impressions is known as an edition. The size of the edition, generally based on the limitations of the printing method, is set by the artist. Because each design produces more than one impression, original prints are often more affordable than one-of-a-kind works of art.

Photographs

Interest in photography has exploded in recent decades. Blockbuster museum shows and the publication of numerous books on the work of contemporary photographers have contributed to widespread awareness and appreciation of the medium. Most photographers issue their photographs in numbered editions, creating a

In the right setting, a large-scale, high-quality print possesses much of an oil painting's grandeur and richness.

A tangerine-colored wall, a sculptural shelf, and matching black frames set off a trio of small black-and-white photographs.

limited inventory in the market. With photography, as with prints, it's possible to build a personal collection without investing enormous sums of money. Excellent images by emerging artists are available for relatively little cost.

Fiber Art

At home on walls and floors, this diverse category encompasses rugs, quilts, tapestries, and even handmade paper. Whatever the materials used or the function intended, fiber art excels at providing warmth and texture. These works come in all sizes, but they are particularly striking in large formats, when they demonstrate their power to transform entire walls.

Other Ideas

From metal or glass wall pieces to ceramic tiles to imaginative woodwork, creative options for walls and floors are too numerous to list. Of course, your choices extend beyond things conceived in an artist's studio. You may already possess an heirloom quilt that begs to be seen in a new way, or a dramatic piece of driftwood gathered on vacation that would look perfect on the dining room wall. Who knows, with assistance, you might be able to turn that unused wallpaper into a floorcloth. It's a matter of expanding your frame of reference. The possibilities are wide open.

With its polished surfaces, clean lines, and uncluttered work areas, this room is all about function. But imagine the space without the wall quilt: every element flat and hard. Not only does the quilt bring a soft and sound-absorbing surface into the room, it adds a twist to the boxy geometry of the built-in shelving. At the same time, the quilt's rich colors add an uplifting note to an otherwise neutral color scheme.

This multilayered silk wall piece reveals a sumptuous side of abstract design.

A pair of prints completes a small seating area. The prints are different sizes and have different frames; however, their shared style and subject matter establish visual continuity.

Arranging
Artwork

Grouped effectively, a focused selection of two-dimensional artwork is greater than the sum of its parts. Images play off one another, allowing a deeper, richer presentation of themes and visual ideas. With a little forethought and a touch of serendipity, you can easily bring together works of art in a way that will bring the walls of your home to life.

Some households possess vast collections of valuable artwork. But you can create artful arrangements even if you own just one or two original pieces and a mind-boggling abundance of family photographs. After all, your home is not a sterile gallery space—you'll find it most satisfying to display the artwork you love in the context of your family life. Before you reach for the hammer and picture hooks, consider the display ideas on the following page.

Four photographs float on invisible wires attached to a sophisticated mounting system. Crisp, matching frames and spot lighting define this dramatic arrangement over a stairwell.

Display Ideas

▪ Mixing family memorabilia such as travel photographs or a child's drawings with works of art can succeed beautifully, even when pieces have different dimensions and subject matter. To give an eclectic arrangement a cohesive look, choose similar uncomplicated frames, perhaps in black metal or pale wood.

▪ On the other hand, images that have something in common, like a collection of woodblock prints or small watercolors, will shine in a variety of unique or ornate frames.

▪ If you prize symmetry, try placing artwork on either side of an imaginary line, in a mirror image arrangement. The centerline could be either horizontal or vertical, depending on the shape of the space you wish to fill.

▪ For a more casual look, align images of different heights along a flat surface, like a mantelpiece or a console table. Mount a few of the images to the wall and let others sit on the designated surface, resting against one another. In this way, an otherwise static grouping gains from a degree of three-dimensionality.

▪ For a cool, restful arrangement that invites a closer look, place small, detailed images in large, simple frames with wide white mats.

▪ Interior designers have a rule of thumb: Uneven numbers of objects are more interesting than even numbers. But, like all rules, this one is made to be broken. One compelling way to present boldly colored abstract works of art is to group four images of the same size in a square or rectangle: two above and two below.

These suggestions are simply starting points. As you begin grouping images, let the artwork, frames and other materials at hand inspire you. Once finished, your arrangements will possess an unmistakable visual and emotional logic of their own.

just *a thought*

I have a small collection of original paintings. Each one admits me to a world that is richer and more brilliant than my own personal experiences. The best artists appeal to the intellect as well as the imagination, and their brushstrokes are imbued with light that is translated into a sense of color.

My living room is illuminated by a Michael Eade fantasy painting that never fails to intrigue me—even at the end of a long, weary day. The relationship between his figures, patterns, and rich colors invites me into a world of sensuality and intuition.

These days, it is difficult to escape the anxious times in which we find ourselves. Where does one turn for comfort? I, like so many others, look to home for solace. More and more, I depend on the paintings I live with to brighten my house and my spirit.

Neither here nor there, hallways are often hurried through. Hang artwork that invites people to pause, linger, and double back for a closer look. In the home's much-traveled common spaces, works of art can be enjoyed by all inhabitants and guests.

Lighting **Two-Dimensional Artwork**

Properly lit, a painting's brushstrokes seem to tremble with energy. An etching's inky lines, pressed into paper, stand out in relief. Appropriate lighting enhances the experience of viewing artwork, bringing color, detail, and evidence of the artist's touch to life.

☐ Two-dimensional artwork on the wall can be lit successfully from a single position, usually with a ceiling-mounted spotlight or a long slender picture light mounted on or above the frame. The goal is to wash the entire piece evenly with light, without allowing much to spill onto the wall or surrounding area. If necessary, you can add a frame over the lens to shape the area of light.

☐ Plan ahead to avoid distracting glare. The angle of light reflecting off artwork covered with glass or thermoplastic always equals the angle of light hitting the surface. Solutions to the problem of glare include: adding parabolic louvers to light fixtures to create a 45° shielding angle, moving ceiling lights closer to the wall where art is displayed, using floor canisters that shine upward, and framing artwork without glass.

☐ Different types of light produce different effects. Incandescent bulbs enhance warm colors like reds and yellows, but flatten cool blues and violets. Halogen bulbs produce strong white light that suits all colors, but they should be used at a low wattage to avoid heat damage. Although they save energy, fluorescent bulbs produce harmful UV rays and should not be used to illuminate artwork.

Learning to using light wisely and purposefully is an essential aspect of displaying two-dimensional works of art. In the process, you will transform and deepen your relationship with the images that fill the walls of your home.

Spot lighting brings out the depth and artistic shading of this ceramic wall divider. Impossible to overlook, this piece reshapes the space around it and ignites the imagination of the viewer.

Finding Neutral Ground

Powerful artwork plays especially well against neutral walls. Neutral colors come in a variety of flavors, from true neutrals—white, black, and gray—to new neutrals that possess a touch of color, like taupe or beige. Although the strength of neutrals is their ability to blend with anything, each one is especially suited to certain combinations of colors and materials, and each can establish a distinctive mood.

White

Pure and pristine, white can run the gamut from fresh and casual to utterly glamorous. White walls, reflecting all the colors in the spectrum, will support and showcase any type of artwork. Paired with crisp white, bold colors and graphic shapes sing. Consider black or clear frames for a strong, contemporary look.

Cream

Cream contains just enough yellow to be uplifting while remaining soft and serene. Cream works beautifully with shades of green, or provides a rich, elegant companion for black-and-white photographs and drawings. Cream walls pair successfully with frames and furnishings in gold tones, oak, or nutty brown wood.

Beige

Sandy beige has quite a bit of yellow in it. It is a natural choice for rooms with honey-toned wood, like oak. Beige is a bit more substantial than airy cream, so it is a great backdrop for artwork in warm, rich colors like rust, orange, or brown, but won't work so well with bright, clear colors. Avoid using stainless steel or aluminum frames—the coolness of bluish-silver metals tends to fight with beige's earthiness.

Taupe

Taupe palettes, whether pale or dark in tone, are calming and sophisticated. Deep purples, blues, greens, and browns take on a velvety lushness against taupe, which is gray with a hint of warm brown. Consider choosing frames in silvery chrome or painted finishes with a touch of shimmering iridescence, but steer clear anything too fiery or yellow, like rust and gold tones.

just *a thought*

From time to time, each of us encounters a room that seems a world unto itself. Everything—artwork, furniture, color, lighting—comes together in such a way that one is immediately transported to another place, as if by magic.

Artists are particularly skillful at helping us weave all the threads together. Witness the work of Barbara Clark, who created this 5 x 9-foot (152 x 274 cm) mural for the foyer of a Florida home. Clark says, "My customers are Italian, and they love the Amalfi Coast, so we selected a photograph of this old villa in Sorrento."

I believe we yearn for enchantment in our lives. At home, we want to walk through inspiring rooms that have emotional resonance and stories to share. In my mind's eye, I enter this Florida home— only to wind up on a beautiful coast in Italy, as if by magic.

Mirror, *Mirror*

From ancient hand mirrors made from polished sheets of metal to the stately hall at Versailles, mirrors have been regarded as objects of wonder and luxury. Today, mirrors are ubiquitous and easily manufactured household objects, yet those created by artists lend special glamour to your décor and offer a perfect reflection of your sense of style. Whatever their origin, you can treat and hang framed mirrors much like other two-dimensional works of art, but a few specific considerations accompany their display.

According to principles of *feng shui*, the traditional Chinese practice and philosophy of achieving harmonious surroundings, mirrors can enhance a home by multiplying and directing its positive energy. But place them thoughtfully! Don't let mirrors reflect anything you don't want more of—such as views of a drab interior or exterior wall, a construction project, or a busy street outside a window. Instead, position mirrors to reflect a pleasant view of your garden, a work of art, or an open door (this is considered auspicious). Feng shui practitioners advise you to think twice before placing a mirror in your bedroom. Mirrors reflect and multiply—and in so doing, they cannot help but stir up extra energy in what is supposed to be your home's most tranquil retreat.

Rhythmic hand carving gives a small mirror outsized graphic impact. Along with a swirling metal stool, the mirror fills a narrow sliver of space with energy.

We think first of mounting mirrors on a wall, but pieces of furniture can incorporate mirrors to stunning effect. Let a mirror-topped table intensify the magic of candlelight or provide another perspective on a beloved object, such as the spectacular underside of a wide glass or ceramic bowl that would otherwise remain hidden from view.

Mirrors are a familiar sight in the entryways of many homes. These mirrors, typically small or narrow, afford a last look at hair or lipstick before heading out the door. Take care to hang such a mirror at an appropriate height. When the tallest person in household stands before it, his or her head and torso should be reflected intact, never cut off at the top.

In a small dining room, a horizontal mirror parallel to the table can bring in additional daylight and create the appearance of a more expansive space. In the evening, when people gather to talk and eat, the mirror will heighten the convivial mood of the gathering as it reflects the table's abundance and the animated expressions of the people seated around it. Try mounting this type of mirror at an angle, with the top several inches away from the wall. This offers the fullest reflection of the activity at the table.

Use a horizontal mirror to open up space above a mantel.

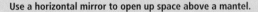

When hanging a mirror, pay attention to the way its position frames views of the rest of the space. The reflection in this fanciful curtain-shaped mirror reveals other metalwork by the same artist across the room.

Styling
Your Floor

A floor is a floor is a floor. That is, until you begin to think of it as something more than a floor. When you think of the floor as a fifth wall, you begin to think of it a little differently. It is still something to walk on instead of lean against, but it, too, is a place for eyes to rest. It is a fundamental part of the room's overall look.

Once you decide that the floor is not merely a bland background for furniture and objects, a new world of possibilities opens up. Train yourself to think of your floors as surfaces available for distinctive works of art. Floor-level artworks, be they rugs, floorcloths, or painted patterns, create boundaries within a room, while adding color and texture to the surroundings. Delicate appearances to the contrary, such floor treatments are designed to withstand daily wear and use, so by all means walk on them!

In the beginning there were rugs. Woven floor coverings have a rich history of serving as items of comfort and symbols of status. The contemporary version of yesterday's rug decorates the floor as well as covers it. Today's fiber artists weave their creative ideas into art for the bottom of the room.

The weaver's artistic sensibilities range from the colorful and exotic to the abstract geometric or to the subtly elegant. Variety of style is matched by variety of technique. Rugs may be hooked, tufted, sheared, sculpted, and even painted. Whatever the method used, the final result is a painting in fiber for the floor.

Imagine hanging a painting on the floor—painted floorcloths open up that possibility. The surface is usually canvas or an equally durable material, and its shape and design can be tailored to the taste of the homeowner. A protective finish ensures that colors will stay true and unmarred for years to come.

If a wall, or even a ceiling, can be painted to make a personal statement, so can a floor. Think of the floor as a canvas for anything including geometric patterns, stenciling, or designs that deceive us into believing that we are walking on marble or exotic woods.

Old wooden floors are prized for their beauty. Today, we can enlist a contemporary woodworker to create inlaid designs that turn a floor into a work of art. Once finished, it can stand alone or serve as a frame for a beautiful rug.

In the artful home, the floor is what you make it, and how you look at it.

In a large entryway, the contemporary leaf design and earthy palette of this rug warms the tile floor while serving as a subtle thematic counterpoint to the rough-hewn wood ceiling above.

Selecting
Floor Coverings

Some plan a room's décor from the ground up, carefully choosing furnishings and accent pieces to draw out the intricate shapes and rich colors of a beloved rug. Others leave the rug for last, hoping to stumble across one that will magically tie all of a room's loose ends together. Either way, here are some ideas to keep in mind:

- When choosing a room-sized rug, interior designers recommend selecting one that leaves eight to twelve inches of floor exposed around the room's perimeter.

- Small area rugs can define a large room's geography and establish intimate spaces for conversation. Generally, the furniture in the grouping should be entirely on or off the rug.

- For a rug beneath a dining table, size it four feet longer and wider than the table to allow ample space for seating.

- Consider commissioning. A high-quality rug is always a significant investment—why settle for something mass produced when, with about the same amount of money and a little extra patience, you can commission a custom rug that will be beautiful and more perfect for your space than you dreamed possible?

A custom-designed floorcloth adapts to a contemporary kitchen, contributing color, pattern, and personality.

This abstract rug anchors a small dining area and pulls together all the colors in the space. In the dining room, make sure the rug is large enough to accommodate chairs even when they are pulled away from the table.

■ Over time, rugs may fade in the presence of strong sunlight—appropriate use of window treatments can mitigate this problem. Some homeowners may even have a protective coating added to their windows to protect the vibrant colors of artwork within. Rotating the position of the rug from time to time can help prevent too much wear in certain spots.

■ Sometimes floorcloths make the most sense. If you are trying to find a durable rug for an office with rolling chairs, a high-traffic entryway, or a place where food is consumed, don't overlook floorcloths. Practical, affordable, and easy to clean, floorcloths offer yet another way to add visual richness to your home.

Guide to the Artful Home, Room *by* Room

A truly artful home nourishes our soul and satisfies our psyche. This life-size work in progress is a place of repose and stimulation, comfort and inspiration. Art lives on the wall above the sofa . . . as well as in the linen closet and under foot. The glass vessel on the coffee table is a beloved and valued piece of art, but so is the table itself, when created by a skilled furniture artist. In the artful home, the ordinary takes a turn for the extraordinary.

Think of the rooms of your home as three-dimensional compositions. Your furniture and furnishings are your materials. From the stage-setting entrance, to private sanctuaries like the bedroom and the bath, to the pure delight of children's rooms and outdoor living spaces, each room reflects different facets of who you are and what you value.

As you work to create a home rich in beauty, consider all of its rooms, first and foremost, as a complete whole. Then, look at the way the rooms relate to one another. Next, focus in on individual rooms. Use furniture to shape rooms within rooms and control the flow within each space. Finally, overlay art and objects that are meaningful to you. When your cherished belongings work in harmony with daily rituals and family life, your dreams and efforts receive their richest reward.

Please read on. As you move from room to room, you'll discover strategies for creating the artful home. *create a home rich in beauty*

Rich in architectural interest, this tiled entryway with vaulted ceilings creates a perfect frame for a collection of accents and furnishings from faraway places.

The Entryway

The mood of your home unfolds at its threshold. A beautiful, inviting entryway ushers visitors into your space and hints at the style of the rooms within. In particular, the artwork you choose to display here sets the stage for your guests and shapes their first impressions of your home. Welcome them with carefully chosen furnishings and works of art.

Consider placing a single sculptural chair in an entry or hallway, where it will stand out as both an art object and a symbol of welcome. Other personal touches, including fresh flowers, a table sculpture, or an antique family photo can complete the artful arrangement.

In the center of a sweeping, high-ceilinged front hall, you may prefer to highlight a round or oval table of generous proportions. Adorn it with a dazzling blown glass vase filled with flowers that can stand up to the room's grand scale. Keep lighting warm and easily adjustable to ease the transition from outdoor light to the composed environment within. For an unforgettable effect, try welcoming dinner guests to an entry illuminated only by candlelight.

Not every entrance affords so much room to play with. Narrow entryways are perfect places for small, framed paintings or prints. The confined space encourages an intimate interaction between the viewer and the art. Small sculptures and objects arranged on a console table can also offer an intriguing introduction to the rhythms of your home. Don't hesitate to change the artwork on display and let it evolve over time.

Whatever its size, do your best to keep your entryway free of clutter and obstructions. In the absence of closets, provide ample shelving and hooks to store coats, hats, shoes, and the like. This high-traffic area of the home calls for a delicate balance of function and grace. It must streamline the routines of everyday life—the daily sorting of mail, removing of coats, and gathering of keys and briefcases. At the same time, it should remind you, each time you step inside, that you have arrived at a cherished place.

In the foyer shown here, a graceful pair of sconces casts a gentle, mood-setting light that softens the transition to the inside. Although the windswept trees of the large, framed print establish a dramatic focal point, the craftsmanship of the hand-carved console quietly steals the show. Accompanying ceramic and blown glass objects complete the entryway vignette with a study in curved shapes and contrasting textures.

The Living Room

The living room, where you gather with family and friends, is the most theatrical space in your home. Think of it as your gallery, your primary space for displaying and enjoying original works of art. Your challenge is to balance the functional needs of the room with a story that expresses something about you—your tastes, your values, your heritage.

Abandon reality for a moment and envision your living room as a clean, empty white space. Now imagine placing your favorite framed artworks and objects in their best possible locations, along with handmade, artist-designed furniture and furnishings chosen to complement the artworks. Of course, in reality you're unlikely to buy new furniture and furnishings to enhance each new piece of art you bring into your home. Still, it can be useful to think about the role artwork would play in your ideal setting.

One common focal point in many living rooms is the fireplace. The mantel and wall above are perfect locations for framed artworks, small sculptures, family photos, or handcrafted candleholders. The artworks you group in this area comprise a still life, a vignette celebrating your own creativity. By refreshing the arrangement periodically—and expanding it to include the entire area surrounding the fireplace—you have the opportunity to seek out new works made by artists: forged iron tools, hand-woven baskets, a rocker, original area rugs. The warmth of this setting is created as much by the artwork as by the fire.

In many homes the living room is the most public part of the home and a hub of family activity. Day-to-day, it is the family's gathering place; on special occasions, it is the setting

An axiom of interior design is that every room needs a bit of black. In this case, a black piano, teapot, and obelisk provide definition and lead the eye through an otherwise airy, light-filled living room.

for entertaining guests. It's almost always the largest room in the home and is usually positioned near the entryway. All of these qualities make the living room an ideal location for displaying large works of art, works that make the living room inviting, yet dramatic and expressive. The size of the room also makes it a flexible space, allowing for a variety of arrangements and focal points.

Splashed with ocean blue, one wall becomes a compelling focal point in a waterfront home with an open floor plan. The accent color makes the black-and-white wall piece pop and ties in with a pair of sofas, the room's largest pieces of furniture.

just *a thought*

It was in Paris, at the Notre Dame Cathedral, that I first fell in love with glass. Traveling through Europe, just out of college, I was too young to have a sense of my own aesthetics. Yet my reaction to the Cathedral's great rose windows was immediate and visceral.

Glass is a magical medium. When used as an architectural element, an entryway door created by an artist can play a key role in how we first experience a home environment. Architectural glass, as it is called, complements the space in which it lives, but it also has the ability to transcend it. The synthesis of light and color has a dramatic effect, simultaneously eclipsing our views and expanding our vision.

Over the years, I've followed my passion and made the acquaintance of artists who explore the integration of glass into the architecture of our homes. In my own home, I have the pleasure of living with French doors by artist Maya Radoczy.

Throughout the ages, glass has been used in places of worship for exaltation and transformation. Our homes are worthy of the same creative attention to light and color. Each of us deserves a daily dose of inspiration.

Stretching from floor to vaulted ceiling, an atmospheric mosaic of
ceramic tile turns a fireplace into a magnificent focal point.

The Significance of the Hearth

A fireplace will inevitably be the focus of any room. It draws eyes in and calls up a host of happy recollections—snow-bound winter nights, long silences punctuated by the snap of blazing logs, stories unfolding over cocoa or glasses of wine.

In bygone centuries, families depended on the hearth for heat, light, and preparing food. Long after we have invented other ways to meet these needs, the fireplace is an object of desire that continues to hold sway over our imaginations. Real estate professionals note that the presence of a fireplace adds to the value of a home.

Reflecting the enduring significance of the hearth, the mantelpiece remains a classic showplace for works of art and family memorabilia. By giving these pieces pride of place, you signal their importance to you. Think carefully about how this focal point can help you express the things you value most dearly. Here are some ideas to spark your imagination.

- A strictly symmetrical arrangement establishes a beautifully formal mood. Try flanking a still life painting with a pair of candlesticks, urns, or small sculptures. Keep this in mind: the more ornate the mantel itself, the simpler you'll want the decorations to be.

- Many mantelpieces are already very linear, often a basic square or rectangle. Let your eye wander outside the box, and approach your mantelpiece and the area around it as a collage or a puzzle of individual pieces. Begin to experiment with the height, texture, color, and materials of the objects you wish to showcase.

More contemporary works of art can work splendidly in traditional arrangements (and vice versa). White accents tie artwork to mantel, while rounded shapes are reinforced in a row of dainty plums, sculpted in bronze.

This painting, cinematic in scale, is an adventurous choice for the band of space between mantel and crown molding.

■ Interesting asymmetrical arrangements give your imagination free reign. A casual grouping can set a different, less formal tone. Enliven your arrangement with clusters of natural objects such as stones. Place a colorful mirror on a mantel next to a collection of seashells. Or arrange glass bottles to hold wildflowers.

■ Add texture with objects that you might not expect to see on a mantel, like a teapot and cups. If you wish to feature a collection of similarly sized objects, you can vary their rhythm by placing some of items on top of wooden boxes or stacks of books.

■ Remember that hanging a single mirror or work of art front and center is not the only way to fill the wall above the mantel. Instead, you can rest an enormous framed print directly on the mantel and let it lean against the wall. Or, create an overlapping display of photographs in a range of sizes.

■ Change or rotate art and objects on a regular basis, or perhaps, with the change of seasons. Whatever you choose to display, make sure it expresses your personality.

■ Finally, if an embarrassment of riches is making your mantelpiece look cluttered, either edit the arrangement or expand the area you have to work with. Bookend the fireplace with shelves—and give yourself even more space for display!

On this mantelpiece, a collection of blown glass bottles and flasks settles into an easy rhythm punctuated by stems of allium.

One **Great Painting**

A great painting demands breathing room. It single-handedly commands attention and, at the same time, asks us to consider its relationship to the furnishings that surround it. Forget about matching the sofa—the painting, a one-of-a-kind work of art, is too important to take a supporting role. Instead, invent ways to play it up. Put a realistic painting in a room with modern furniture, for example. Or surround a painting of strong colors with neutral furnishings. Your personal style reveals itself most clearly in the dramatic tension between the artwork you choose and a room's functional pieces.

In this living room, a large abstract painting establishes an elegant mood. Against its horizontal bands of color, the graceful lines of traditional furnishings stand out in clear relief.

A realistic painting is a striking addition to a large, rugged fireplace in a mountain home. The high-ceilinged space calls for large-scale artwork, easily read from a distance.

Colors found elsewhere in the room emerge with heightened intensity in this contemporary painting. Singled out by an unexpected blaze orange frame, the painting strikes a joyful note against subdued sea-foam green walls.

Lighting can make or break the mood of a dining room. This handsome two-lamp fixture is perfectly tailored to both the height of the ceiling and the proportions of the table below.

The Dining Room

To be healthy, our souls need regular nourishment. The main source of this replenishing experience is the world we build inside our homes. The dining room and dining room table, in particular, serve this essential purpose, not just with delicious meals, but with the tableware, candles, music, and wine that accompany the food. The best dining rooms are those that lead us to linger over coffee and dessert.

Just as you strive to please guests with your hospitality and menu selection, so should you choose artworks that encourage a convivial mood. The dining room is an ideal setting for art that elicits a meaningful story. Guests will notice the work displayed in the room and ask you about it. Sharing a unique story about the artist or about how you acquired the work reveals something about your interests and gives your friends a more complete sense of who you are.

A traditional dining room has much to gain, for example, from the addition of a contemporary piece of art, which can serve as a counterpoint to the weightiness of the dining room table. On the other hand, a modern dining room is softened by placing a handmade rug or floorcloth under the table. The room is personalized with antiques and folk art.

New trends in cooking and eating have introduced new ways of entertaining at home. But the time-honored standards for beautiful presentation are still with us. Flowers are the table's crowning glory, especially when a beautiful vase is used—a floral arrangement lends color and texture, and completes the visual effect.

Today's artists have created a bounty of beautiful, useful objects for the table. They are re-creating our tables, our gathering places, and showing us that function can be, should be, an artful blend of utility and beauty. There is the handmade dinnerware that has the look and feel of museum pieces but is dishwasher safe. And there are metal salt and pepper shakers, ceramic coffee cups, and wooden cooking utensils that fit the hand and please the eye. It is not enough that the objects we use at the tables where we eat and meet do the things they are intended to do. They should have some character and spirit as well—they should be a reflection of the people who use them.

just *a thought*

My favorite dinner guests arrive early and stay late. It is the best of friends who pitch in to help chop the salad or volunteer to set the table. I let them select which set of handmade dishes to dine from; their choices of colors and arrangements are always so wonderful and uniquely different from mine.

My favorite dinner table is filled with the work of talented artists who combine the artistic with the functional in each individual piece. A variety of styles in handcrafted dinnerware— from contemporary and elegant to colorful and zany—allows us to express our creativity beyond the food we serve. We're lucky to have so many artists today creating complete place settings, along with an exciting range of beautiful serving pieces, flatware, and stemware.

My dining room is the center of my universe. It is there that I launch my engagement with the larger world, both social and spiritual. In this small piece of real estate, I re-connect with family and old friends, and discover the pleasure of new friends.

Living well means different things to different people. For me, the simplest pleasures of the home are the most satisfying.

Light filters into a comfortable bedroom, revealing how everyday objects can be beautiful, soulful, and thoroughly functional.

The Bedroom

Your bedroom is your inner sanctum, a quiet haven for intimacy and reflection. Since the bedroom is a private space, it invites introspection and expressiveness. Surround yourself with things you love. Begin and end each day in a room that sustains your soul.

Here more than anywhere, perfection should be the least of your concerns. Ease, simplicity, and honesty are the keynotes for a space where you can fully relax and be yourself. Forget about complex arrangements or design by the book.

Instead, start with the basics: comfort and warmth, soft light, a peaceful refuge from the day's demands. You could bask in the gentle light from a handmade paper lampshade. Nestle in a chair that loves your body, upholstered with fabric woven from a rainbow. Dream in a bed that supports your spirit as well as your back. Dress at a mirror that cradles your reflection with joy. Wake to artwork that speaks to your heart.

To create a sense of peace, the clutter must go. However, too much tidiness makes a room rigid. A pile of ironing will fray your nerves, but a tumble of books by your bed may delight you. If so, find a fabulous lamp to spotlight the books, and corral stray clothes into a beautiful hamper. Wardrobes, chests, and boxes gather up your goods, give a room structure, and can be wonderfully expressive.

Having established calm and order in your bedroom, you should make room to dream. This is where original artwork can truly shine. Paintings or prints might spark romance, invoke serenity, or invite leisurely contemplation. Treat the souvenirs of your inner life to a little extra breathing room, and display only those things that you can count on to make you smile. These might be favorite photos of loved ones, flowers from your garden, or objects gathered on your travels.

This bedroom's furnishings and decorative accents lie low beneath an uplifting mural. With the addition of an architectural fragment and a framed drawing, a sketchy detail in the artwork becomes a full-fledged visual theme.

just *a thought*

Years ago, furniture artist Craig Nutt and I attended college together. (He was a hippie, and I wasn't.) We've been close friends for most of my adult life. I have had the pleasure of watching Craig's career develop and blossom; today he is recognized as one of the stars in the field of studio furniture.

So it was a big deal when, a few months ago, my husband and I decided to purchase Craig's *Onion Blossom Table.* This piece adds beauty and personality to our home, but more importantly, reminds us daily of a long-standing friendship that has enriched our lives.

My personal feelings about this table reflect a national movement to know more about the sources of the things we buy and live with. (Nowhere is this more evident than the local farmer's market, where we meet and greet the farmers who grow our food.) There is great satisfaction in owning something made by the hand of an artist one knows.

An artist-made bed makes a wonderfully personal statement. This headboard is incised with expressive hieroglyphs.

As you think about artworks for the bedroom, begin by considering the bed itself. Furniture makers will be happy to show you photographs of bed frames made for previous clients or discuss a unique design specifically for you. Bedside tables, lamps, and wall sconces are also special when made by an artist. Like wood, fiber is very much at home in the bedroom. Tapestries or art quilts can create a strong visual impact and provide a practical benefit by softening sounds.

As you begin to design the retreat of your dreams, trust your senses and give your imagination free rein.

Luscious color fills a bedroom that strikes a balance between simplicity and opulence.
Above the bed, a sculpture of purple plum branches casts artful shadows. Its form seems
to move and change with the light, animating the space.

The Bathroom

No other room reflects universal lifestyle changes more than the bathroom. From humble beginnings, it has become the place where we pamper ourselves. The luxurious bath is definitely here to stay.

There are striking ways to add your personal signature to your home's most private space. There is a wealth of artwork in ceramic, metal, and glass that will hold up beautifully in the dampness of a bathroom. Imagine custom mosaics, ceramic tiles, or a stunning glass sink.

Borrow art ideas from other rooms in your home. Hand-painted ceramic canisters for the kitchen might make perfect containers for bath salts, cotton balls, or extra soap. A wood quilt rack could be just the thing for displaying towels.

Nearly every bathroom has a mirror—this is your chance to make a statement. Rip out that standard-issue mirror and replace it with a remarkable work of art. Choose something with an unusual shape or imposing proportions. Let it reflect your personal sense of style as well as pretty faces.

Like all of the rooms in your home, even the cleanest and most utilitarian bathroom will benefit from the creative mark of an artist.

The creator of this vanity believes that every element of a building can be re-created as a work of art. Incorporating aluminum, stainless steel, and stained glass, this striking piece blurs the line between sink and sculpture.

A ceramic sink makes colorful use of a tight corner space.

Bronze fittings and marble tile complement faux finishes and trompe l'oeil, creating a luxurious bathroom sanctuary.

just *a thought*

Recently, at a friend's party, I ducked into the small powder room and discovered there a wonderful surprise—a handmade glass sink crafted by an artist. It reminded me, once again, that the smallest detail is an opportunity to delight.

It is the care and attention to details that turns a home into a sanctuary for living. My friend's powder room sink was personal and thoughtful, a welcoming gesture to visitors as well as a form of self-expression.

William Morris, the father of the Arts and Crafts movement, said, "We should have nothing in our homes that we do not know to be useful or believe to be beautiful." His statement, made near the turn of the century, was a call to arms then, and rings just as true today. In fact, his ideal is even more meaningful in an age where technology routinely trumps beauty in the objects of everyday life.

I'm sure Morris would agree that it is the details of one's home, especially those associated with the humble necessities of daily living, that heighten our appreciation of life. In attending to the details, we make every day a holiday and turn the ordinary into the extraordinary.

Regarding
Furniture

Next to the structure itself, furniture is the most fundamental, the most considered, and the most used part of the home. While decidedly functional, furniture pieces can provide significant opportunities for individual expression.

To the casual observer, furniture design appears to be dictated by certain basic requirements. Chairs need legs and backs, tables have to be elevated from the floor, beds should be horizontal, cabinets need shelves at least and probably doors as well. And yet furniture designers and manufacturers continue to surprise us with their originality. It's astonishing that chairs, tables, and beds can have so many variations and still meet the single, great, overarching criterion: providing comfort for the human body.

Because furniture is so important in the home, it's easy to justify splurging on a very special piece that you would love to own. Save your decorative superlative for the rooms that will be seen the most—the living or dining rooms—or the place it will give you the most pleasure, such as the bedroom. Either way, one outstanding furniture piece can make a room look infinitely better than the sum of its parts.

Mirror images in warm mahogany, these benches complete a circular space at the top of a stairway.

A cherry console with a sweep of brushed aluminum steps into a prominent place behind a sofa, greeting all who approach the fireplace and offering its surface to other works of art.

This dynamic showcase for favored objects reinterprets the classic cabinet form in sinuous, richly patinated steel fitted with glass windows and shelves.

An artist approaches the ABCs of furniture design with fresh ideas, inventive techniques, unexpected materials, and a sculptor's eye and view of the world. The reasons, then, to seek out artist-made furnishings are many and wondrous. Choose a single handcrafted piece to draw attention and make a clear statement about your sense of style, or create harmony out of a group of unique pieces.

There is an element of surprise in artist-made furniture. Quirks of personality reveal themselves in sensuous curves and spiraling movement. These curves can't be manufactured (woodworking equipment, after all, requires straight lines). These curves must be made by hand. Art, like nature, is hardly ever straight. It is often apt to be warped and wavy, twisted, irregular, and fragmented.

Furnishings speak to us, set the moods for our rooms, and make our lives brighter and better. At its best, each piece extends comfort even as it expresses something true about its owner and its maker. As you shape your personal environment, seek inspiration in furniture that dances about the room. Such pieces demand that we set them out and let them speak for themselves.

Architectural **Details**

A painting here, a small sculpture there. At home, far from the exalted spaces of museums and galleries, it's easy to think of art as an add-on or a finishing touch.

However, many artists team up with homeowners to create works that are integral to the spaces they inhabit. Windows, doors, walls, floors—each element defines a home's structure and directs the flow of light or foot traffic.

"But my home is what it is—I don't have the luxury of designing it from scratch," you object. Don't let your home's perceived limitations define you! There is no reason to mask elements you don't like under layers of furnishings and other things you do like.

It can be tremendously satisfying to take a fresh look at what lies beneath it all and make a few imaginative leaps. Unique doors transform a space. Stained glass windows introduce brilliant color. Murals or tiles applied directly on the walls give a room a new point of view. A handcrafted railing or gate lends its environment unexpected ingenuity.

Your home's basic structure holds many possibilities for personal expression—look for ways to turn it into a fitting frame for a more artful life.

A hearth surrounded by intricately sculpted bas-relief gives this home an unmistakable sense of place.

Two sets of pocket doors provide light and levity to an interior residential hallway. In addition to designing and creating architectural details for the home, many artists are familiar with architectural and building codes, allowing them to provide the additional service of installing work in your home.

just *a thought*

More and more these days, I find that my spirit needs a refuge. A friend's struggle with a serious illness affected me deeply this past year. It caused me (extrovert that I am) to seek solitude and time for reflection.

Walks in the woods are best, but a few special places in my home also serve the purpose of inviting quiet reflection. Here, away from the sound of the phone and television, I can allow myself the luxury of deeper thoughts, as I ponder the questions we all begin to face at a certain point in our lives.

Feng shui, the Chinese discipline of harmonious energy, speaks to the ways our environments affect physical, emotional, and spiritual well-being. I imagine an ancient Chinese master smiling as I settle into my favorite chair with a cup of tea and a good book by my side. It doesn't really matter if I read, so long as I feel comfortable and comforted.

And the book on the table beside the chair? My personal recommendation is Thomas Merton's *Thought in Solitude*, from which I quote: "When society is made up of men who know no interior solitude, it can no longer be held together by love...."

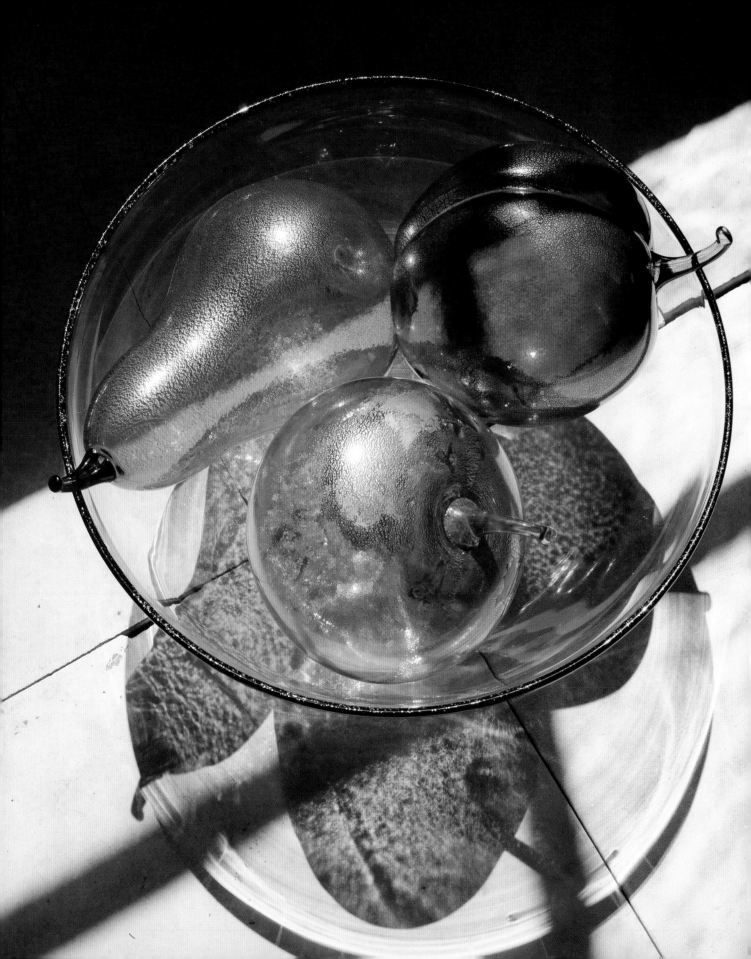

Acquiring *and* Protecting Artful Objects

Now that you're inspired to bring original artwork into your home, you may be thinking, "But where do I find these wonderful works of art?" and "How do I care for them once I bring them home?" The answers to these practical questions are as varied as the objects you're looking for.

Your search for artwork can take many forms. It can be direct and methodical, as when you're looking for a print or painting to pick up the colors in your living room, or organic and adventurous, as when you're searching for a special something to mark a milestone anniversary. It can be the focus of a month of weekend outings to galleries, art fairs, and artist studios, or an evening of online browsing.

If you have a very specific artwork design or style in mind, you might consider commissioning a piece directly from an artist. Custom-designed works of art can reflect your personal taste and vision. If you enjoy the involvement with an artist that an art commission requires, this is the ultimate way to buy original art.

No matter how you acquire your works of art, you'll want to ensure that these family treasures will last for years to come. Most pieces will stand the test of time and require little maintenance (though you should always ask the artist for care instructions). There are, however, a few basic tenets for maintaining artwork to keep in mind.

But first, let's go shopping for artwork!

searching for a special something

Finding Art

When the urge to personalize your home takes hold, contemporary artists stand ready to satisfy your desire for the unusual, the unique, and the handcrafted. Their work can be purchased online or through galleries and retail shops. Artists often sell work directly too, either at craft fairs or right out of their studios.

Here are some points to consider when looking for artwork through these specific channels.

Developing a relationship with a favorite art gallery can be an efficient and appealing way to find artwork that suits your personal style.

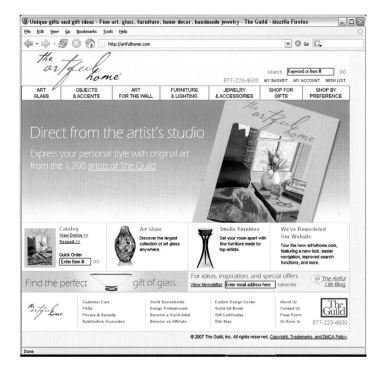

Internet Shopping

A virtual gallery offers distinct benefits, especially if you're pressed for time, prefer to shop at night, or want to see a very broad selection of quality artworks. Internet technology allows you to search for art items meeting precise specifications, and you can typically access artist credentials with a click of the mouse. Finally, packaging and shipping are handled by these online galleries, which know better than anyone how to get fragile pieces to you safely.

Online shopping does have certain limitations, however. For example, don't try to estimate the size of an artwork based on a thumbnail image; instead, crosscheck the listed dimensions against a ruler.

Galleries

Purchasing or commissioning a work of art through a gallery provides the benefit of consultation: you're tapping into the expertise of the gallery staff and the relative assurance that the work meets high aesthetic and professional standards. Galleries may also provide additional services, such as in-home consultation, framing, or even artwork loans that let you live with a piece before you buy. Galleries often have special knowledge of particular artists—or access to artists whose work is not available elsewhere. The gallery's ability to negotiate with their artists may save you time, money, and legwork.

The phone book for your area probably includes a listing like "Art or Craft Galleries." Be prepared to find a wide range of businesses, because the word *gallery* may be used to describe everything from framing shops to retail stores. A true gallery presents changing exhibits and represents a stable of artists, though showrooms and retail stores may also have much to offer as well.

Develop a habit of attending gallery openings in your city or town. When the artwork you see appeals to you, introduce yourself to the gallery owner. Discuss your interest in purchasing art and the kinds of work you're attracted to. Be sure to mention your budget—and don't feel intimidated if you don't want to spend a great deal of money. Galleries are always looking for new clients, and they'll be happy to spend time getting to know you.

Art Fairs

Depending upon the crowds and the weather (if the art fair is outdoors), attending art fairs can be great fun—and a good way to see the work of many artists at one time. Most art fairs are juried, so you can expect to meet artists who work at a professional level.

Art fairs typically have websites that will provide you with a list of participating artists, parking information, art fair hours, and related special

just *a thought*

In the beginning, you fall in love. It starts in your feet and pretty soon it's in your chest and then your throat and finally you're thinking about it all the time.

That's what happened to me when I first spotted the photography of Terry Allison online. This talented artist captures cloud-laden skies in dramatic black-and-white imagery. And there is one piece, *Dunes of Destin*, which immediately stole my heart.

I grew up in a small town in South Alabama, only 90 miles from Destin, Florida. Allison's photography captures the brilliant white sand and rolling sand dunes of my youth. Destin will always be my favorite beach, no matter how old I am and how far I travel.

The association with memories is a constant theme with so many of the things that we surround ourselves with, whether it's treasured family silverware or a quilt passed down from generations past. Intuitively, we seek out objects and artwork that have meaning and connection for us. In the process of gathering, we re-connect with the people and times that have made us who we are today.

This particular piece of artwork serves as a bookmark in my journal of memories. I am in love; I must have it.

events. You may want to bring a small notebook so you can take notes, and be sure to wear comfortable shoes for lots of walking and standing.

If an artist whose work you like is busy with other customers, come back when he or she is less busy so you can talk about the work you like—or would like to commission. Most artists have printed materials available so you can read more about their work, education, and experience; contact information should be included so you can get in touch later, if that's more convenient.

When a piece of artwork interests you, don't be shy about asking the artist how the piece was made or what materials were used in its creation. Or share with the artist what you like about the piece. This is an easy way to strike up a conversation, and most artists enjoy talking about their work.

Artist Studios

When you visit an artist's studio, you're treated to a behind-the-scenes look at where and how the artwork you're bringing into your home is created. This adds another, very rewarding layer to your appreciation of a piece. A visit to an artist's studio also provides the benefit of immediacy. Many artists keep at least a few completed works in the studio and can provide overnight turnaround for last-minute gifts and the like. This is most often true with artists who make small-scale works, but even artists who produce large-scale paintings or furniture often keep a few available pieces on hand.

Rules of common courtesy apply during your visit. Be sure to call ahead: the artist may have limited visiting hours, especially during crunch times. Once you're there, don't overstay your welcome. Enjoy your visit but recognize that the artist will need to get back to work.

Some communities offer organized tours of artists' studios on a particular day or weekend each year. These open-studio events are terrific opportunities to meet artists and learn about the processes they use.

Shop Creatively

No matter where you shop for original works of art, remember that your search is really only limited by your imagination. If you don't see what you're looking for right away, it may be time to consider a commission.

A visit to an artist's studio gives you a chance to see the artist at work, inspect artwork at close range, and, best of all, ask questions.

Commissioning Artwork

Commissioning a work of art is not as intimidating as it may sound; in fact, it can be tremendously fulfilling to participate in the process of designing your own environment. Instead of choosing something made, among things that exist, you get to choose a maker, a style, an idea, a concept.

There are several ways to find the right artist for your project: First, make your initial selection on the basis of what you like about the artist's work that you have seen in person or in print. (Don't, however, expect to see the exact piece you're looking for. Remember you're choosing an artist at this point, not a piece of artwork.) Look for creativity and command of the materials or technology, while considering how the work might fit your specific environment.

Once your A-list is narrowed down to two or three names, it's time to contact the artists. Be prepared to provide information about the piece of artwork you're looking for, your budget, and even the materials and colors you have in mind (if, indeed, you do have those in mind). As you talk, try to determine the artist's interest in your project and pay attention to your comfort level with the artist. Be thorough and specific when asking questions. Is the artist excited about the project? Will your needs be a major or minor concern? Has he or she worked on projects of similar size and scope?

If you feel like you might have trouble working together, take heed. But if all goes well, ask the artist for a list of references. These are important testimonials, so don't neglect to make the calls. Ask about the artist's

Commissions like this pendant lamp can provide that missing something in a room. The rounded edges in this piece provide softness to this dining room, at a size and wattage fully scalable to the homeowner's needs and tastes.

Commissions can provide a unique spark for the home in an unexpected place. This mural warms up a neutral wall in a typically unadorned residential space, the staircase.

work habits and communication style, and—of course—about the success of the artwork. You should also ask if the project was delivered on time and within budget. If you like what you hear, you're one important step closer to hiring your artist.

Most artists charge a design fee whether or not they're ultimately hired for a project, so start by asking for sketches from your top candidate. If you're unhappy with the designs submitted, go to your second choice. If, on the other hand, the design is what you'd hoped for, it's time to finalize your working agreement with this artist.

A signed contract or letter of agreement commits the artist to completing his or her work on time and to specifications. It also assures the artist that he or she will get paid the right amount at the right time. Customarily, artists are responsible for design, production, shipping, and installation. If someone else is to be responsible for installation, be sure to specify who will coordinate and pay for it.

The more complex the project, the more you should budget for the artist's work and services. With larger projects, payments are usually tied to specific milestones; these serve as checkpoints and assure that work is progressing in a satisfactory manner. Payment for larger commissions is customarily made in three stages: (1) upon signing the contract (which includes the development and production of a design), (2) midway through the project, and (3) when the work the work is delivered or installed. If the commission is cancelled at any point, the artist keeps the money already paid for work performed.

All of this may seem a little formal for what is a personal collaboration, but it is well worth the extra effort. The result will be a piece of artwork made to your specifications and liking, as well as a reflection of your personality and spirit.

Determining Value

When we find art that appeals to us, our reaction is immediate. We fall in love first—and then think about the pragmatic aspects of buying and owning it. Before you hand over your credit card or sign a commission agreement, ask yourself a few hard-nosed questions. Do I want to live with this work for years to come? If I buy it, where will I place it in my home? And, equally important, is the piece worth the asking price?

The cost of a work of art is often related to the experience of the artist. Those who have worked in their fields for many years command higher prices than relative newcomers. The same is true for artists whose work is included in museum collections or publications, or who

This earthenware horse was created in a limited edition of seven, which increases its marketplace value. In addition, the artist has garnered solo exhibitions, awards, and has work in the collections of major corporations, all of which help to establish her as a serious and credible artist whose work should increase in value.

have mounted one-person shows. These are landmark events: they demonstrate respect for the artist on the part of curators, publishers, and gallery owners, and they have a cumulative effect on the artist's prices.

Here are some other things to look for:

◼ Education. An artist's academic record sheds light on his technical background and skills. Don't base your choice of artist on education alone, however. Some of our most esteemed artists developed their skills as apprentices or within an artist's community rather than an institution.

◼ Exhibition history. Emerging artists compete to participate in group shows at local and regional galleries; artists who are more advanced in their careers mount solo exhibitions at well-known galleries and museums. These are important reference points for the value of their work.

◼ Reviews. Art critics act as interpreters, and their reviews not only evaluate the quality of the artworks, but also place them in the context of history and genre. A strong endorsement in a respected publication can have a significant influence on an artist's career.

◼ Collections. It can be affirming to learn that others share your passion for a particular artist. If his work is part of a museum collection—or is owned by prestigious collectors and corporations—this adds to the value.

◼ Career overview. When you meet artists or gallery owners, ask them to comment on the artist's body of work, refinement of themes and techniques, and artistic influences. The answers will provide insight into the artist's depth of experience, thus influencing the value you place on the work.

Although the factors discussed here relate to marketplace value, they should also be considered as you think about the value you and your family place on a work of art. That said, your passion for a work of art should always drive your purchase. The right surroundings and appropriate placement in your home environment are much more important than investment appeal. This is one area where I urge you to lead with your heart.

If you yearn to collect large-scale pieces, consider outdoor sculpture for the garden. The natural setting will free you to choose more eclectic artwork than your home's interior could accommodate.

This pair of patinated metal vases may be the beginning of a collection of vases, round objects, or metal works for the mantel. A single piece can launch a fun collection you never knew you wanted!

Collecting
Artful Objects

We are what we eat, physically. We are what we read, intellectually. And we are what we collect, aesthetically. The urge to gather and display is universal, and today's artists are providing us with an abundance of wonderful pieces—from the purely utilitarian to the emphatically decorative—that give us more and more ways to satisfy that universal urge.

A collection starts with a single piece, and it need not be an expensive or taxing process to add to it. There are many affordable art forms out there. One-of-a-kind or limited-edition pieces can be acquired with a minimal budget. Prints, ceramic teapots, or even small architectural details such as drawer pulls or tiles are just a few of the ways you can incorporate original works of art into your home with relatively little damage to your wallet.

As a reflection of your memories, dreams, joys, and personal beliefs, a collection can also be based on the metaphysical; a favorite color, theme, idea, or place can inspire an assemblage of varying artworks.

However you define your collection, remember to educate yourself about your purchases along the way to develop a greater appreciation for the media contained within. Visit museums and galleries to see examples of pieces you may want to add to your collection. If you're collecting blown glass vessels, for example, you may want to take a glassmaking course or workshop to enhance your appreciation even more.

If you're collecting works from a single artist, consider the artist's entire range of work, and select a piece based on either its originality in relation to the body of work as a whole or as the finest example of that artist's output.

Ultimately, a collection is a collection because it is yours, not because it is composed of fixed pieces by particular artists. So find those pieces that reflect your personality best, and enjoy watching your collection grow.

Obtaining Documentation

Aside from its obvious aesthetic and emotional appeal, art can be a sound investment—but only if you document it. When you purchase a work of art, ask if a Certificate of Authorship is available. This document certifies the artist's authorship, the title of the piece, dimensions, date of purchase, and current market value of the artwork. Keep it in a safe place for future reference and insurance purposes.

To further protect your investment, you may also want to keep the following information on file:

■ Receipts associated with the artwork purchase or maintenance

■ Photographs of the piece

■ An accurate description, including dimensions

■ A copy of the artist's resume

A well-documented piece of artwork provides peace of mind and simplifies the process of appraising or donating the work at a later date.

just *a thought*

Do you think eleven teapots are a little excessive? My husband certainly thinks so, but me—I'm not so sure.

My personal philosophy is that once you own more than three of anything, you suddenly have a collection, which then gives you permission to add to that collection. Selectively, of course.

I am attached to each of my eleven teapots, and I swear they are attached to me as well. I lovingly arrange and rearrange them on my shelves, where they keep one another company.

Eleven feels like enough until the day I spot a new teapot that seems made for me and me alone. A psychic craving sets in. This happened to me the moment I spotted Suzanne Crane's *Kettle Teapot*, shown at the right below. Its twisted, vine-like handle is in perfect proportion to the feet and spout. It is both elegant and accessible, and it really wants to be mine.

I haven't purchased it yet, but there is lust in my heart. Sooner or later, I will carefully broach the subject with my husband, and somehow convince him that living with a dozen teapots makes perfect sense.

Care and Maintenance of Your Artwork

A major benefit to owning an artist-made piece of work is knowing that it was created with care and attention to detail that doesn't apply to pieces coming off the assembly line. Some handmade creations, including woven floor coverings, porcelain dinnerware, and custom tables and chairs, must be used (and, at times, abused) on a daily basis to fulfill their functions in the home. Although original works of art are made with durability and longevity in mind, there are a few simple things you can do to enhance your artwork's life span.

What follows is a medium-specific list of basic tips for artwork care. (Always remember, however, to ask the artist or gallery representative for maintenance recommendations specific to the piece you're purchasing.)

Ceramics

Though a relatively hardy medium, ceramic pieces may crack, chip, or break if handled or used improperly. A ceramic sculpture, if displayed in an enclosed cabinet or case, will be protected from dirt and dust. If you need to clean your ceramic piece, consult its glaze. Unglazed pieces can be brushed with a soft makeup brush or paintbrush—or sprayed with canned air. Glazed pieces are best washed in lukewarm water and a gentle soap. (You may want to line your sink with a towel or rubber mat in case it slips!) Extreme fluctuations in temperature or humidity can be harmful to delicate pieces; likewise, even oven-safe stoneware dishes should not be placed directly into a hot oven. Instead, allow the dish to heat up along with the oven.

Glass

Use care when handling glass works—and two hands! Make sure your hands are clean, but don't wear gloves, which may be too slippery. Avoid lifting glass pieces from handles, spouts, or other protruding elements. How you clean your piece may depend on the type of glass from which it's created. Cast glass is best simply dusted with a soft brush. Glass lighting may be cleaned with a basic glass cleaner—just make sure to clean it when it is at room temperature. Glossy blown glass can be wiped with a soft cloth moistened with vinegar and water, or any other non-abrasive cleaner.

There's no need to tread lightly on artisan floor coverings, which are meant to handle the wear and tear of daily life. Take care, however, to keep these fiber treasures out of the sun's direct light. Glass pieces shine in this well-lit room divider and require only minimal dusting or cleaning as needed.

Fiber

To ensure they receive proper air circulation, many fiber works are generally left unframed. Fiber wall hangings benefit from limited handling and an occasional vacuuming, using a gentle attachment, to keep them free of dust. Consult the artist about the best way to hang the piece—it's often best to attach a fabric sleeve to the back and mount it using a wooden slat or rod. Use soft, cool lighting near these pieces to prevent the breakdown of individual fibers. Fiber floor coverings may be spot cleaned with a commercial cleaner (it's best to ask the artist for a recommendation) or cleaned professionally as needed. Limit direct sun exposure to all fiber pieces in order to prevent fading or discoloration.

With only minimal care required, metal artworks for the home are a durable decorating option, and in the case of this steel fire screen, may serve a functional role by protecting or supporting their environment.

Outdoor pieces, such as this bronze fountain, are made to last for many years. Check with the artist or gallery, however, about how to best care for your piece's surface treatment, which may require periodic cleanings or re-applications of protective coatings or waxes.

Metal

Whatever their surface treatment, metal works are often finished with a protective wax, lacquer, or paint. If your metal piece is outdoors, its surface may need protection from pollution, dirt, and natural elements. Ask the artist what kind of changes you can expect so you won't be surprised later on, and have him guide you to the best protective strategy. Indoors, metal pieces or architectural elements can be cleaned with an oil-based polish and then buffed with a dry rag. Bronze, however, should only be dusted with a lint-free cloth or feather duster. For heavier bronze cleaning, use distilled water, then dry the piece thoroughly.

Paintings

Painters apply everything from watercolors to oil paints—or sometimes an unusual combination of several media—to a wide variety of surfaces. Most should be framed without glass, which means they are highly susceptible to their environments, particularly to sunlight. Pastels are the exception, and they should be framed only under glass (thermoplastic has a magnetic pull.)

Oil paintings are quite durable provided they have been properly varnished. (They can even withstand touch, which makes them a nice option for children's rooms.) Keep oil paintings clean by wiping them gently with a damp cloth. Because the oil is impervious to water, you won't damage your artwork. Acrylic paintings, by contrast, should be dusted lightly with a soft brush.

Photographs and Prints

Works on paper are generally more delicate than works on canvas and should be framed behind glass. Be sure your framer uses acid-free, archival materials to ensure no harm comes to your artwork. Frame photographs and prints behind glass if you're worried about scratches; use thermoplastic for a lighter-weight alternative. Use a lint-free cloth to clean either surface, and be sure to spray cleaning solution on the cloth—not the piece itself. Ultraviolet protection and anti-glare options are available. Also, avoid hanging photographs in direct sunlight or in settings that are very humid. These conditions can cause your artwork to fade or ripple.

Think of contemporary artworks as the heirlooms of tomorrow, and ensure their preservation appropriately. Good care from the beginning will guarantee that your art treasures will be passed on for future generations to enjoy.

The care of a painting depends entirely upon its particular medium, so be sure to check with the artist or gallery. Also, use common sense when placing your painting, which should be removed from environments of direct sunlight, extreme changes in humidity, or strong fumes.

In Conclusion

I've always been obsessed with interiors and, in particular, the world we create inside our homes. I believe our personal spaces shape us as much as we shape them. Objects gathered on life's journey become building blocks for homes that are forever works in progress. Among my favorite discoveries are things made by artists, those immensely talented individuals who inspire, teach, and share their gifts so generously.

Each new year I craft my resolutions, with a focus on filling my life and home with personal expressions that bring not only physical but also psychological sustenance. In the spirit of new beginnings, I share those resolutions with you:

- Live with what you love, and collect what you crave, as these objects will help you create your own personal landscape.

- Turn the ordinary into the extraordinary by surrounding yourself with beautiful, useful things. Luxury is not measured by price, but by the amount of attention lavished on the details.

- Trust your instincts, and make your own choices about the things you want to live with.

- There are no rules, so don't be afraid to make mistakes.

- Slow down, and enjoy the process of getting there.

- If it doesn't make you happy, change it. Life is short.

- Sate your thirst for color on a regular basis.

- Learn about the artists whose work speaks to you, about their inspirations, and their techniques and processes. Connect with the value system that sparked their creations.

- Use the handmade teacup as a metaphor for how central original artwork can be in your life. Hold it in your hands, appreciate its beauty, and reflect upon it.

- Fill your home with joyful creativity, artwork, artful objects, and spirit that enlarges your own.

Toni Sikes

Art Glossary

Acrylic. A water-soluble paint made with pigments and synthetic resin; used as a fast-drying alternative to oil paint.

Alabaster. A fine-textured, usually white, gypsum that is easily carved and translucent when thin.

Aluminum. A lightweight, silver-colored metal used extensively in commercial applications, and occasionally by metal artists. In a process called *anodizing*, aluminum is given a tough porous coating that can be colored with dyes.

Appliqué. A technique whereby pieces of fabric are layered on top of one another and joined with decorative stitches.

Aquatint. Printmaking process used to create areas of solid color, as well as gradations of white through black tones. Usually has the appearance of transparent water color.

Bas-Relief. Literally, *low-relief.* Raised or indented sculptural patterns that remain close to the surface plane.

Batik. A method of applying dye to cloth that is covered, in part, with a dye-resistant, removable substance such as wax. After dyeing, the resist is removed, and the design appears in the original color against the newly colored background.

Beading. The process whereby decorative beads are sewn, glued, or otherwise attached to a surface.

Beveled Glass. Plate glass that has its perimeter ground and polished at an angle.

Bonded Glass. Glass pieces that have been adhered together by glue, resin, or cement.

Brass. An alloy of copper and zinc. Brass is yellow in color, and though harder than either of its constituents, it is appropriately malleable for jewelry making.

Bronze. Traditionally, an alloy of copper and tin widely used in casting. The term is often applied to brown-colored brasses.

Burl. A dome-shaped growth on the trunk of a tree. Intricately patterned burl wood is often used by wood turners and furniture makers.

Casting. The process of pouring molten metal or glass, clay slip, etc., into a hollow mold to harden. Some casting processes permit more than one reproduction.

Celadon. French name for a green, gray-green, blue-green, or gray glaze produced with a small percentage of iron as the colorant.

Ceramics. The art and science of forming objects earth materials containing or combined with silica; the objects are then heated to at least 1300°F (704°C) to harden.

Chasing. A technique in which steel punches are used to decorate and/or texture a metal surface.

China Paint. A low-temperature overglaze fired onto previously glazed and fired ceramic.

Dichroic Glass. A thin metallic coating on any type of glass. The coating is applied at a high temperature in a vacuum chamber.

Die Forming. The process of placing metal between two steel dies or stamps and squeezing them together under high pressure. This process shapes and strengthens the metal.

Digital Imaging. Refers to the creation, manipulation, and production of images by use of computer technology, including software and printers.

Diptych. Artwork on two panels that are hung together. Historically, a hinged, two-paneled painting or bas-relief.

Earthenware. Ceramic ware with a permeable or porous body after firing (usually to a temperature of 1600°F to 1900°F [871°C to 1038°C]).

Embossing. A decorative technique in which a design is raised in relief.

Enameled Glass. Glass decorated with particles of translucent glass or glass-like material, usually of a contrasting color, which fuses to the surface under heat. Multicolored designs can be created, as well as monochrome coatings.

Engraving. An intaglio printing process in which a design is incised into a metal plate. Characterized by sharp, clean lines and high definition. Also called line engraving.

Etched Glass. Glass decorated, carved, or otherwise marked by sandblasting or the use of hydrofluoric acid. The glass is partially covered with an acid-resistant wax or gum and the exposed area is etched.

Etching. A printing process in which chemical agents are used to deepen lines drawn onto a printing plate.

Firing. Heating clay, glaze, enamel, or other material to the temperature necessary to achieve a desired structural change. Most ceramics are fired in a kiln to temperatures ranging from 1600°F to 2300°F (871°C to 1260°C).

Forged. A blacksmithing technique in which metal is shaped by hammering, usually while at red or white heat.

Fuming. A vapor deposition process in which a thin film of metal (usually silver, platinum, or gold) condenses on the surface of a hot piece of glass or clay, resulting in an iridescent surface.

Fused Glass. Glass that has been heated in a kiln to the point where two separate pieces are permanently joined as one without losing their individual color.

Giclée. French term meaning *sprayed*. A process by which an image is rendered digitally by spraying a fine stream of ink onto archival art paper or canvas. Similar to an airbrush technique.

Glassblowing. The process of gathering molten glass onto the end of a blowpipe and forming it into a variety of shapes by blowing and manipulating it as the glass is rotated.

Glaze. Glassy melted coating on a clay surface. Glaze has a similar oxide composition to glass, but includes a binder.

Gouache. An opaque watercolor paint, or work so produced. Gouache is applied like watercolor, but reflects light due to its chalky finish.

Hue. The pure state of any color.

Ilfochrome. A trademarked photographic paper and the process of making prints with such paper. Ilfochrome prints are produced from slides or transparencies, not color negatives.

Impasto. A thick, uneven surface texture achieved by applying paint with a brush or palette knife.

Incalmo. The glassblowing technique used to create horizontal or vertical bands of color by forming and connecting cylinders of colored glass.

Inclusions. Particles of metal, bubbles, etc., that occur naturally within glass or are added for decorative effect.

Inlay. A decorating technique in which an object is incised with a design, a colorant is pressed into the incisions, and the surface is then scraped to confine the colored inlay to the incisions.

Intaglio. A printmaking process in which an image is created from ink held in the incised or bitten areas of a metal plate, below the surface plane. Engraving, etching, mezzotint, and aquatint are examples of the intaglio process.

Iridized Glass. Flat or blown glass sprayed with a vapor deposit of metal oxides for an iridescent finish. The iridized layer, which resembles an oil slick, can be selectively removed for a two-tone effect.

Iris Print. The trademarked name for a digital print produced by an Iris Graphics inkjet printer. (See "Giclée.")

Kiln. A furnace for firing clay, forming glass, or melting enamels; studio kilns can achieve temperatures up to 2500°F (1371°C) and can be fueled with gas, wood, or electricity.

Kiln-Forming. A glass-forming process that utilizes a kiln to heat glass in a refractory or heat-resistant mold, slump glass over a form, or fuse two or more pieces of glass together.

Kinetic. Active kinetic sculpture has parts that move, whether by air currents (as with a mobile) or by motors and gears.

Laminated. Composed of layers bonded together for strength, thickness, or decorative effect.

Lampwork. The technique of manipulating glass by heating it with a small flame. An open flame is advantageous in very detailed work.

Leaded Glass. Glass containing a percentage of lead oxide, which increases its density and improves its ability to refract and disperse light. Leaded glass is used for ornaments and for decorative and luxury tableware.

Limited Edition. Artworks produced in a deliberately limited quantity. All items in the edition are identical and each one is an original work of art. The limited size of the edition enhances the value of each piece.

Linocut. A relief print process similar to woodcut. Wood blocks covered with a layer of linoleum are carved with woodcut tools, coated with ink, and printed by hand or in a press.

Lithography. A planographic printmaking process based on the repellence of oil and water and characterized by soft lines and blurry shapes.

Low-Fire Glazes. Low-temperature ceramic glazes, usually associated with bright, shiny colors.

Luster. A brilliant iridescent film used on ceramic glazes; formed from metallic salts.

Majolica. An opaque glaze, usually white, with a glossy surface. Typically decorated with bright overglaze stains.

Marquetry. Decorative patterns formed when thin layers of wood (and sometimes other materials, such as ivory) are inlaid into the surface of furniture or other wood products.

Mezzotint. An intaglio printing process that produces areas of tone rather than clean lines.

Monoprint. A print produced by painting directly onto an already-etched surface and printing the image by hand onto paper.

Monotype. A print made when an artist draws or paints on a glass or metal plate and then prints the image onto paper.

Mosaic. The process of creating a design or picture with small pieces of glass, stone, terra cotta, etc.

Murrini. A small wafer of glass bearing a colored pattern. Formed by bundling and fusing colored glass rods together and then heating and pulling the resulting cylinder to a very small diameter. When cut into cross-sectioned wafers, each piece bears the original pattern in miniature.

Oil Paint. A paint in which natural oil—usually linseed—is the medium that binds the pigments.

Palladium. A photographic process in which the image is produced by palladium crystals deposited on the paper.

Pastel. A crayon of ground pigment bound with gum or oil. Pastel crayons have varying ratios of pigment to chalk and gum; the more pigment, the more intense the color.

Pate de Verre. A paste of finely crushed glass that is mixed, heated, and poured into a mold.

Patina. A surface coloring, usually brown or green, produced by the oxidation of bronze, copper, or other metal. Patinas occur naturally and are also produced artificially for decorative effect.

Photoetching. A printmaking technique in which a light-sensitive metal plate is exposed to photographic film under ultraviolet light.

Photogravure. A printing process based on the production, by photographic methods, of a plate containing small ink-receptive pits.

Polaroid Transfer. A trademarked name for the process by which an image recorded by the camera's lens is reproduced directly onto a photosensitive surface, which functions as both film and photograph.

Porcelain. A clay body that is white, strong, and hard when fired. When sufficiently thin, it is also translucent.

Print. An image made from an inked surface. Prints are usually, but not always, produced in multiples.

Raku. The technique of rapidly firing low-temperature ceramic ware. Raku firings were used traditionally in Japan to make bowls for tea ceremonies.

Relief Print. A process in which a print is produced from the relief carving on a metal plate or a wood or linoleum block.

Repoussé. An ancient process in which sheet metal is hammered into contours from both the front and the back.

Reverse Painting. A technique where paint is applied to the back side of a surface (typically glass) and viewed through the front. This process requires the painting to be done in reverse order; what appears closest to the viewer as a detail or highlight must be painted first rather than last. Any lettering must likewise be painted in the mirror image so it will appear right facing when viewed from the front.

Salt Glaze. A glaze created during high-temperature firings. Sodium, usually in the form of rock salt, is introduced into the fully heated kiln and forms a clear coating on the clay, often with an orange-peel texture.

Sand Casting. An ancient and still widely used casting method in which moistened sand is packed against a model to make a mold—usually for metal.

Sandblasting. A method of etching the surface of a material by spraying it with compressed air and sand.

Sepia. Warm, reddish-brown pigment produced from octopus or cuttlefish ink, used in watercolor and drawing ink. In photography, some toning processes produce a similar color in the print.

Silkscreen Printing. A printing process in which paint, ink, or dye is forced through a fine screen onto the surface beneath. Different areas of the screen are blocked off with each layer of color. Also known as *serigraph*.

Silver Gelatin. A photographic process that uses silver halide crystals suspended within the photographic emulsion to produce the image. The most popular type of black-and-white photograph produced today.

Slumped Glass. Preformed flat or three-dimensional glass that is reheated and shaped in a mold.

Spalted. Wood that contains areas of natural decay, giving it distinctive markings. Spalted wood is used for its decorative effect.

Still Life. A depiction of a group of inanimate objects arranged for symbolic or aesthetic effect.

Stoneware. A gray, red, or buff clay body that matures (becomes nonporous) between 1900°F and 2300°F (1038°C to 1260°C).

Terra Cotta. Low-fired ceramic ware that is often reddish and unglazed.

Terra Sigillata. A thin coating of colored clay or clays applied like a glaze. A terra sigillata solution is composed of fine particles of decanted clay and water.

Triptych. A three-paneled artwork. Historically, triptychs were hinged together so that the two side wings closed over the central panel.

Turned. Wood or other materials shaped by tools while revolving around a fixed axis, usually a lathe. Cylindrical forms (dowels, rungs) and circular designs (bowls) are made in this way.

Trompe L'Oeil. Literally, *fool the eye* (French). An object or scene rendered so realistically that the viewer believes he or she is seeing the real thing.

Vitreograph. A print made from a glass plate that has been prepared by sandblasting or etching.

Vitreous. Clay fired to maturity, so that it is hard, dense, and non-absorbent.

Watercolor. Watercolor paints are made with pigments dispersed in gum arabic and are characterized by luminous transparency.

Whiteware. A generic term for white clay bodies.

Woodcut. A relief printing process in which a picture or design is cut in relief along the grain of a wood block.

Artist
Credits

Pages 2-3
Dina Angel-Wing, sculptures and teapot; Michael Cohn and Molly Stone, bowl

Page 5
Alicia Berger of Grand Image, print; Natalie Blake, ceramic vessels; Tracy Glover Studio, lamp; Andrew Muggleton, end table; Mary Lynn O'Shea, chair; Emi Ozawa, clock; Joël Urruty, sculpture; Laura Zindel Ceramics, cup and saucer

Page 6
The Chatham Glass Co., vase

Pages 6-7
Joseph Hyde, photographs; Richard Jones, ikebana vases; Whitney Smith Pottery, ceramic vessel; Mike Wallace, blue vase

Page 8
Hubbardton Forge, sconce; Courtesy of Tom Kirby/Winterowd Fine Art, painting; Dorset Custom Furniture, desk

Page 10
Beth Ozarow, sculpture

Page 12
Darlis Lamb Studio, pear sculpture; Peet Robison, vase; Janna Ugone & Associates, sconce

Page 13
Curtis Benzle, sculptural lighting

Page 14
David Moose, painting

Page 15
© Heather Gentile Collins, All Rights Reserved, www.gentiledesigns.com, painting

Page 16
Brian Kershisnik, print; Monique LaJeunesse, Little River Hotglass Studio, jack set; Cheryl Williams, sculpture

Page 17
The Chatham Glass Co., glass sculpture; John Maggiotto, print; Mitch Ryerson, chairs; Erik A. Wolken, table/stool

Page 18
Eric J. Bladholm, glass lamp; Mary Hatch, painting; Kelsey Sauber Olds, Beam Fine Furniture, table; Judith Weber LLC, tea set

Page 19
Basa Projects, LLC, rug; Benjamin Moore Inc., cobalt vase; Charles W. Palmer, painting; Dick Weiss, self-portrait vessel (floor)

Page 20
© Johniene Papandreas/Courtesy Gallery Voyeur, Provincetown, MA, painting

Page 21
Carla and Greg Fillippelli, basket; Don Green, footstool; Lisa Jacobs, vase; Steven Kozar, prints; Brad Smith, bench; Alan Vaughn Studios, floorcloth

Page 22
Rebecca Cross, mural; Chris Horney, table and mirror

Page 23
Robert Spielholz and Kathleen Hargrave, vase

Page 25
Carol Green Studio, jars; Marlies Merk Najaka, print; Whitney Smith Pottery, vase

Page 26
Joe Gurkoff, print

Page 27
Kathy Erteman, bowl; Walter Kravitz, painting; Jamie Robertson, table

Page 28
Diana Harrison, table lamp; David Joyce Studio, painting; Monique LaJeunesse, Little River Hotglass Studio, jack set; Michael F. Pilla, stained glass; Janusz Poźniak, pitchers

Page 29
Patricia Burling/Willowweave, rug; Jim Byrne, painting (end of hallway, center); Jamie Harris Studio, vessel (on table); David Kiernan, table; Jack Moulthrop, vessel (floor)

Page 30
Aristides Demetrios, sculpture

Page 31
David Coddaire, cabinet; Marie E.v.B. Gibbons, ceramic sculptures; Claudia Mills, wall hanging/runner; Mary Lynn O'Shea, chair

Page 33
Kent Floeter/Stephen David Editions Ltd, collage

Page 34
Mollie Massie, Myers Massie Studio, Inc., chair (right); Rachel Miller/Timothy Miller, chair (left); Rab Terry, floorcloth; Barbara Zinkel Editions, print

Page 35
Brian Kershisnik, print; Kinzig Design Home, lamp; Andrew Muggleton, table; Robert Wilhelm, bowl

Page 36
© Heather Gentile Collins, All Rights Reserved, www.gentiledesigns.com, painting

Page 37
Joan Kopchik, wall hanging

Page 38
Robert Longo, drawing

Page 39
Michael Bauermeister, vessels; Andreas Charalambous, print

Page 40
Scott Grove, table; Tim Harding Studio, wall hanging; Michael Jones, ceramic stool; Bernard Katz Glass, vessel

Page 41
Peter Karner, bowl; Jan Schachter, casserole and creamer/sugar set

Page 42
Larry Zgoda, door

Page 43
Nancy Gong, Gong Glass Works, glass light wells

Page 44
Tommie Rush/Tomco Studio, bowl

Page 46
Aristides Demetrios, sculpture

Page 47
Natalie Blake, vessel; Kevin Earley, table; Marlies Merk Najaka, print

Page 48
Nicholas Kekic, bottles; Melanie Newlon, painting; Rick Sherbert, hanging lamps, vase, and bowl

Page 49
Kathy Cooper Floorcloths, floorcloth; © Maxwell MacKenzie, photograph

Page 50
Andrew Muggleton, bed and end table

Page 51
MML Textiles, pillows

Page 52
Mark Del Guidice Furniture, console; Hubbardton Forge, wall torches; Lost Angel Glass, vase; Webb Tregay Studio, print

Page 53
Marcie Jan Bronstein, print; Marie E.v.B. Gibbons, sculpture; Pamela Joseph, mural

Page 54
Courtesy of artist Sam Gilliam, painting

Page 55
Gadi Efrat, Sculptor; sculpture (right side of mantle); Gaya Glass, fluted glass bowl and plate; Ivan Reyes, painting

Page 57
Dierk Van Keppel Glass Artist, vases

Page 58
Robert Mickelsen, sculpture

Page 59
Dewey Garrett, vessels; John Kingsley, table; Peter Mangan, hanging lamp

Page 60
Emily Pearlman, bowls

Page 61
Bennett Bean, vessel; Meryl R. Berger, sculpture

Page 62
Susan Madacsi, sculpture

Page 63
Nicholas Bernard, ceramic vessel (bottom left); Christian Burchard, three baskets; Jack T. Fifield, wood vessel (top left); Carol Green Studio, lidded jar; Carol McFarlan, oval vase; Elida and Joe O'Brien, yellow teapot; Vicki Reed, photograph; JoAnne Russo, cactus basket; Richard Swanson, teapot and teabowls (top center); Kerry Vesper, star bowl; Candone Wharton Sculptural Ceramics, white jar; Cheryl Williams, bowls (center and center right)

Page 64
Helen Vaughn Studio, painting

Page 65
John Hein, desk

Page 66
Craig Easter, tray; Julie and Ken Girardini, metal shelf; Kliszewski Glass, glass vessels; Sokolhohne.com/714-606-7396, painting

Page 67
Natalie Blake, vessels; Ken Elliott, print; Blaise Gaston, table; Martin Kremer, bowl; Liora Manne, pillow

Page 68
Al Allen/Greg Thompson Fine Art, painting (left); Jonas Gerard, painting (right); Robyn Horn, turned wood

Page 69
Josephine, photograph

Page 70
Natalie Blake, lidded vessel (left); Carol Green Studio, lidded vessels (center); Maeve Harris of Grand Image, print; Richard Judd Furniture, tables; Studio Paran, glass vases; Jim Webb, lamp

Page 71
Dina Angel-Wing, sculptures and teapot

Page 72
RichardLeeWhitehead.com, paintings

Page 73
Christine Dell, ceramic pieces; Color Musings, scarf; Hubbardton Forge, lamp

Page 74
RobertHolmesSculpture.com, sculpture

Page 75
Myra Burg, wall pieces; Christopher Gryder, mural

Page 76
Nicholas Wilton/www.nicholaswiltonpaintings.com, painting

Page 78
Natalie Erwin, painting

Page 79
CB Glass, vase; Max Hayslette of Grand Image, print (bottom); John May, lamp; Cheryl Williams, bowl; Diane Williams/Greg Thompson Fine Art, painting (top)

Page 80
Marilyn Henrion, wall quilt; Stephen Perrin Fine Woodworking, shelf (top); Vicki Reed, photographs (top)

Page 81
The Chatham Glass Co., glass vessels (foreground); David Coddaire, wavy cabinet; Tim Harding Studio, wall hanging; Darlis Lamb Studio, pear sculpture; Mary Lynn O'Shea, chair; Studio Paran, glass vases (background); Eric Ziemelis, console table

Page 82
Carrie Crane, prints; Jeremy Cline, sculptures; JV Newcomb Designs, chair; Erik A. Wolken, stool/table

Page 83
Andreas Charalambous, photographs

Page 84
Michael Eade/www.michaeleade.com, painting

Page 85
Rebecca Cross, paintings (left wall); Raye Leith, painting (far wall)

Page 87
Elizabeth MacDonald, mural

Page 88
Arthur Stern Studios, Benicia, CA, www.arthurstern.com, window

Page 89
Dorset Custom Furniture, desk; Hubbardton Forge, lamp; Courtesy of Tom Kirby/Winterowd Fine Art, painting

Page 90
Victor Chiarizia, vessel (bottom); M. Ellen Cocose, mixed-media wall hangings (top, left wall and above mantle); Edda M. Jakab, prints (bottom); Kerry Vesper, console table (bottom)

Page 91
Barbara L. Clark/Clark & Hall Studios, painting

Page 92
Beverley Ashe, print; Curt Brock, vase; Jenna Goldberg, mirror; Lisa Jacobs, stools; Bob and Laurie Kliss, vessels; Rab Terry, floorcloth

Page 93
Bennett Bean, vessel; Contour26/ Designed by Eitan Kleiner, mirror (top); Carol Green Studio, candleholders; Kimberly Winkle, mirror (bottom)

Page 94
Joan Weissman Studio, rug and vase

Page 96
Patricia Dreher, Designer/Painter, floorcloth

Page 97
Barbara Barran/Classic Rug Collection, Inc., rug

Page 99
Pat Flynn, cuff bracelet; John Kingsley Furniture, mirror; Kinzig Design Home, lamp; Nancy Templeton/Takota, wood box

Page 100
Joe Gurkoff, prints

Page 101
Anthony Biancaniello, fruit sculpture; Mark Del Guidice Furniture, console; Carol Green, lidded vessels; Hubbardton Forge, wall torches; Daniel Slack, vase; Helen Vaughn, print

Pages 102-103
Courtesy of artist Sam Gilliam, painting; McKay Scheer Studio LLC, sculpture (left); Michael Sherrill, teapot

Page 104
Libby Ware Studios, wall sculpture

Page 105
Maya Radoczy, doors

Page 106
Kari Lonning, basket; Elizabeth MacDonald, ceramic tiles

Page 107
Kathleen Ash/Studio K, sconces; Maeve Harris of Grand Image, print; Darlis Lamb Studio, sculpture

Page 108
© Johniene Papandreas/Courtesy Gallery Voyeur, Provincetown, MA, painting

Page 109
Studio Paran, vases

Page 110
Art © Kenneth Noland/Licensed by VAGA, New York, NY

Page 111
Joe Andoe, painting (top); Aurelio Grisanty, painting (bottom)

Page 112
Andrew Berends, vessels; Maea Brandt, painting; Hubbardton Forge, hanging light

Page 113
Strini Art Glass/Lighting, dinnerware and stemware

Page 114
Klara Borbas, round vase (left, background); David Coddaire, pedestal; Ken Elliott, print; Pamela Hill, quilt; Chris Horney, console table; Claudia Mills, runners; Keith Raivo, chest; Brad Smith, bed and bedside table; Pablo Soto, vessels (on console); Janna Ugone & Associates, clocks; Holly Wallace, vase (left table) and lamp

Page 115
Dana S. Westring, painting

Page 116
Priscilla Cypiot, table (right);
Mark Del Guidice Furniture, bed;
Craig Nutt, table (left); Rosetree
Glass Studio, vase; Jill Schwartz/
Elements, clock

Page 117
Sticks and Stones, wall sculpture

Page 118
Patrick L. Dougherty, sink,
countertop, vessel and cups
(right); Frank Santoviz, vanity
and mirror (left)

Page 119
Imago Dei/Custom Murals,
Decorative Painting, Fine Art,
Public Art, plaster and mural

Page 120
Joseph Thompson, Bear Creek
Glass, sink

Page 121
Douglas W. Jones, benches

Page 122
Natalie Blake, vessel (on console
table); Cohn-Stone Studios, vessels
(on mantel); Michael Jones, ceramic
stool; Darlis Lamb Studio, pear
sculpture; Melanie Leppla, lamps;
Meg Little/On the Spot, rug; Millea
Furnishings, pillows

Page 123
John Suttman/Suttman Studios,
cabinet

Page 124
Mark J. Levy/Mark Levy Studio,
doors; Kevin Yee Studio, fireplace

Page 125
Andrew Muggleton, chaise and table

Page 126
Anthony Biancaniello, centerpiece

Page 128
A. Andrew Chulyk/Studio
Maxima, wood boxes; Random
Orbit, can vessels

Page 129
Terry L. Allison, photograph

Page 130
Glass artist Josh Simpson

Page 131
Wendy Hybl Fannin, drawings;
Hubbardton Forge, pendant lamp

Page 132
Dana S. Westring, mural

Page 133
Jeri Hollister, sculpture

Page 134
Diana Reuter-Twining, sculpture

Page 135
David M Bowman Studio, vases

Page 136
Marko Spalatin, prints

Page 137
Christine Dell Ceramics, teapots
(bottom left and center); Suzanne
Crane, teapot (bottom right and
right-hand image); Peter Karner,

teapot (top left); Judith Weber LLC,
tea set (top right); Laura Wilensky,
teapot (top center)

Page 139
Patricia Burling/Willowweave, rug

Page 140
Mollie Massie/Myers Massie Studio,
Inc., fire screen; Rosetta, sculpture

Page 141
Walter Kravitz, painting

Page 142
Darlis Lamb Studio, sculpture

Page 145
Larry Halvorsen, bowl

Page 146
Larry Zgoda Studio, window

Page 149
Pieper Glass, goblets

Page 151
Lynn Basa, rug

Page 152
Dierk Van Keppel Glass Artist,
hanging lamps

Page 155
Peter Trumbull Crellin Studio
Furniture, chair, table, and mirror;
Cheryl Wolff, teacups

Page 156
Christine and Michael Adcock, wall
piece; Carol Green Studio, vessel and
candleholders

Page 157
Pearl River Glass Studio, doors;
Mario Villa, Inc., vase

Design
Professional
Credits

If you would like the benefit of creative collaboration on your own home, consider contacting design professionals such as those listed here, all of whom graciously contributed images of their artful designs to this book.

In particular, we would like to thank Mary Douglas Drysdale, one of the premier interior designers in North America today. Examples of her designs appear throughout this book. These interior spaces resonate with taste and style, each one a distinctive integration of her three passions: art, architecture, and decoration.

Mary Douglas Drysdale
2026 R Street Northwest
Washington, DC 20009
drysdaleinc@netzero.com
tel 202-588-0700
fax 202-588-8464
pages 27, 38, 54, 102-103, 141

ARKANSAS
Greg Thompson Fine Art
Little Rock, AR
www.gregthompsonfineart.com
pages 68 (left), 79 (top)

CALIFORNIA
Vicki Blakeman Interior Design, Inc.
Westlake Village, CA
www.BlakemanInteriors.com
pages 55, 66

Jan Gunn Designs
Orinda, CA
www.designfinder.com/gunn
page 100

Stacey Lapuk Interior Design Group
San Rafael, CA
www.staceylapukinteriors.com
pages 111 (bottom), 117

Turner Martin Design
Palo Alto, CA
www.turnermartindesign.com
page 72 (interior design)

Randall Whitehead, IALD
San Francisco, CA
www.randallwhitehead.com
page 72 (lighting design)

COLORADO
Charles Cunniffe Architects
Aspen, CO
www.cunniffe.com
page 111 (top)

DISTRICT OF COLUMBIA
Andreas Charalambous, AIA, IIDA
Washington, DC
www.formaonline.com
pages 39, 83

Cunningham + Quill Architects
PLLC
Washington, DC
www.cunninghamquill.com
page 85

Mary Douglas Drysdale
Washington, DC
drysdaleinc@netzero.com
pages 27, 38, 54, 102-103, 141

MARYLAND
Jonas Carnemark, CR, CKD
Bethesda, MD
www.carnemark.com
page 69

NEW JERSEY
Art Forms Gallery
Red Bank, NJ
ArtFormsGalleries.com
page 128

NEW YORK
BHR Design
New York, NY
bhrdesign@aol.com
page 110

Shields & Company Interiors
New York, NY
shieldsint@aol.com
pages 33, 61 (left)

Photo Credits

Eric Ferguson
White School Studio
242 N. Lexington Street
Spring Green, WI 53588
www.whiteschoolstudio.com
tel: 608-588-3331
*Pages 5, 6, 6-7, 10, 12, 16, 17, 18
(both), 21, 25, 29 (bottom), 31,
34 (left), 35, 40, 41, 44, 47, 48
(bottom), 51, 52, 53 (bottom), 57, 59
(bottom), 60, 62, 63, 66 (top), 67,
70 (both), 79 (bottom), 80 (top), 81,
82, 90 (bottom), 92, 93 (bottom), 99,
101, 107, 109, 114, 116 (top), 122,
126, 133, 135, 136, 137 (both), 140
(top), 142, 145, 149, 155, 156*

Maxwell MacKenzie,
Architectural Photographer
2641 Garfield Steet NW
Washington, DC 20008
www.maxwellmackenzie.com
tel: 202-232-6686
fax: 202-232-6684
*Pages 22 (right), 38, 49 (top right),
69, 85, 115, 132*

Dan Abbott, *page 58*
J. Addington, *page 73 (left)*
Terry L. Allison, *page 129*
Dennis Anderson Photography,
page 72
Susan Andrews/SGA Photography,
page 146
Gary Bardwell, *page 130*
Michael Bauermeister, *page 39 (right)*
Gordon Beall, *page 49 (bottom)*
Bennett Bean Studio, *page 61 (right)*
Barry Blau, *page 75 (right)*
Frank C. Brants, *page 78*
Brewster Commercial Photography,
page 64
Richard Bruck, *page 42*
Misha Bruk, *page 100*

Ari Burling Photography, *pages 29
(top), 139*
Clark & Hall Studios, *page 91*
M. Ellen Cocose, *page 90 (top)*
www.ChrisConroyPhotography.com,
page 111 (bottom)
Billy Cunningham Photography,
page 110
Lydia Cutter, *page 48 (top)*
Patrick L. Dougherty,
page 118 (right)
Michael Eade/
www.michaeleade.com, *page 84*
Stephen Funk, *page 9*
Jonas Gerard, *page 68 (right)*
Marc Golub, Courtesy of the City of
Shaker Heights, OH, *page 108*
Larry Dale Gordon, *pages 30, 46*
Christopher Gryder, *page 75 (left)*
Joe Gurkoff, *page 26*
Soo-Yeon Han, *pages 55, 66 (bottom)*
Geoffrey Hodgdon, *pages 39 (left), 83*
Jrabinowitz.com, *page 94*
Russell Johnson Photographer,
Seattle, WA, *pages 19, 151*
Pamela Joseph, *page 53 (top)*
Kingensmith, *pages 15, 36*
Andrew D Lautman, *pages 27, 54,
102-103, 141*
Oded Löbl, *page 93 (top)*
John Lucas, *page 116 (bottom)*
Gary Mamay, *page 37*
David O. Marlow, Aspen,
page 111 (top)
Jack McCarty, *page 104*
www.NormanMcGrath.com, *page 87*
Rob Melnychuk, *page 34 (right)*
Andrew Miller, *page 74*
David Moose, *page 14*

Kevin Muggleton, *pages 50, 125*
© Daniel A Newcomb, *page 20*
Brent Nicastro, *pages 49 (top left),
65, 105*
Mary Noble Ours, *page 154*
Jennie Oppenheimer, *page 76*
Pearl River Glass Studio, Inc.,
page 157
Tom Petrillo, *page 13*
Tim Pott Photography, *page 152*
Jessica Potter, *page 128*
Russell Powell, *pages 68 (left), 79 (top)*
Howard Lee Puckett, *page 120*
© Robert Reck, *page 123*
Diana Reuter-Twining, *page 134*
Steve Schneider/Photography,
page 28
Mel Schockner, *page 140 (bottom)*
Schopplein.com, *page 96*
Paul Schraub, *page 113*
William Seitz Photography, *page 106*
J.D. Small, *page 43 (both)*
Robert Spielholz, *page 23*
Arthur Stern, *page 88*
Ann Stratton, *pages 33, 61 (left)*
Studio Place, *page 22 (left)*
© John Sutton Photography 2007,
page 117
Szalon Antiques/J. Hoffman, *page 97*
Susan Teare, *page 121*
Ken Wagner Photo, *page 80 (bottom)*
Jeremy Wells, *page 119*
Jim Westphalen, *pages 8, 73 (right),
89, 112, 131*
Frank Wing Photography,
pages 2-3, 71
Lloyd C. Wright, *page 118 (left)*
Kevin Yee Studio, *page 124 (right)*
Jamie Young, *page 59 (top)*
John G. Zimmerman, *page 124 (left)*

Acknowledgments

Home decorating books are a dime a dozen, so it was incredibly wonderful to connect with Carol Taylor, President & Publisher of Lark Books, who shared my belief that there was a need for a very different kind of book. I am ever grateful for her vision and support throughout this project.

Lark Books seems to be filled with the best professionals one could hope to work with. Valerie Shrader, editor extraordinaire, truly cares about words and their meaning. She exhaustively went through the manuscript and made gentle suggestions for improvements that were right on target. Kristi Pfeffer designed a book that was even more beautiful than I had imagined. The fact that she accomplished this under impossible timelines is even more amazing.

Jill Schaefer and Melita Schuessler served as my editorial and creative team at The Guild, and the fact is that the book wouldn't exist without their talent and Herculean efforts. Jill guided the editorial process from start to finish; her outstanding organizational skills kept us all on track. Melita's beautiful writing and editing made me sound much better than I deserve.

Mike Baum, The Guild's President, shouldered many additional responsibilities while I was giving birth to this book. He did this with his usual good spirit, and for that I am grateful. My visionary Board of Directors also gave this project their full support and encouragement.

My husband, Bill Kraus, has lovingly taught me the meaning of partner in business and in life. He patiently read the drafts, looked at the layouts, and never ever complained about the many weekends lost to writing.

And lastly, I want to thank the artists, the people who have overwhelmed me with blessings, making me rich with friendships. The work of artists fills this book and our lives with creativity and inspiration.

Index

A

Acknowledgments, 157

Acquiring and Protecting
   Artful Objects, 126–141

Adding a Showstopper, 74–75

Adding Texture and Material, 40–41

Alcoves and Niches, 68

Allison, Terry, 129

Appreciating Geometry, 42–43

Architectural Details, 124

Arranging Artwork, 83–88

Art Fairs, 129

Art Glossary, 143–147

Artist and Designer Credits, 148–153

Artist Studios, 130

Art of Composition, The, 24–43

Art of White Walls, The, 54–55

B

Balance, 29

Bathroom, 118–120

Bedroom, 114–117

Bringing Walls to Life, 78–82

C

Care and Maintenance of Your
Artwork, 138–141

Ceramics, 138

Character of Color, The, 44–55

Chests and Side Tables, 68

Coffee Tables, 67

Collecting Artful Objects, 135–136

Color coordination, 16, 18–19,
  44–55

Commissioning Artwork, 130–132

Conclusion, 142

Consoles and Hall Tables, 66

Crane, Suzanne, 137

Creating Vignettes, 32–35

D

Decorating Creatively, 62–63

Decorating Walls and Floors, 76–97

Decorative Objects, 60

Design Professional Credits, 154–155

Determining Value, 133–134

Developing a Personal Style, 12–14

de Wolfe, Elsie, 35

Dining Room, 112–114

Displaying Small Treasures, 73

Dressing Your Home's Intimate
Spaces, 58–61

E

Emphasis, 28

Entryway, 100–101

Establishing Relationships, 64–65

Exploring Color: A Primer, 50–53

F

Feng shui, 92–93, 125

Fiber, 139

Fiber Art, 80

Finding Art, 128–130

Finding a Focal Point, 36–38

Finding Neutral Ground, 89–93

Floor, 70

Functional Objects, 60

G

Galleries, 129

Glass, 105, 138

Glass sinks, 120

Guide to the Artful Home, Room by
Room, 98–125

H

Hearths, 106–109

I

Internet Shopping, 128

J

Just a Thought journal entries, 14, 23, 26, 35, 49, 53, 61, 63, 73, 84, 91, 105, 113, 116, 120, 125, 129, 137

L

Lamps and Lighting, 59, 72, 86–87

Learning to See, 15–19

Lighting Artwork and Objects, 72

Lighting Two-Dimensional Artwork, 86–87

Living in Color, 46–49

Living Room, 102–111

Living with Beautiful Objects, 56–75

M

Mantels, 107–109

Memory tapestries, 36

Merton, Thomas, 125

Metal, 140

Mirrors, 92–93

Morris, William, 120

N

Negative space, Using, 31

Nelson, George, 62

No Mere Seat, 34

Nutt, Craig, 116

O

Obtaining Documentation, 136

One Great Painting, 110–111

Opportunities for Display, 66–72

Other Ideas, 80

P

Paintings and Drawings, 78, 140

Patterns, 22

Pedestals, 71

Photo Credits, 156

Photographs, 79, 141

Playing with Scale, 39

Prints, 79, 141

Proportion and Scale, 30

R

Radoczy, Maya, 105

Regarding Furniture, 121–125

Rhythm, 29–30

S

Sculpture, 58

Selecting Floor Coverings, 96–97

Shelves, 66

Styling Your Floor, 94–95

T

Take Your Time, 20–22

Think Like an Artist, 20–23

U

Understanding Design Principles, 26–31

Use My Art, 17–19

W

Windowsills, 70

V

Variety, 26–27

Vessels, 59